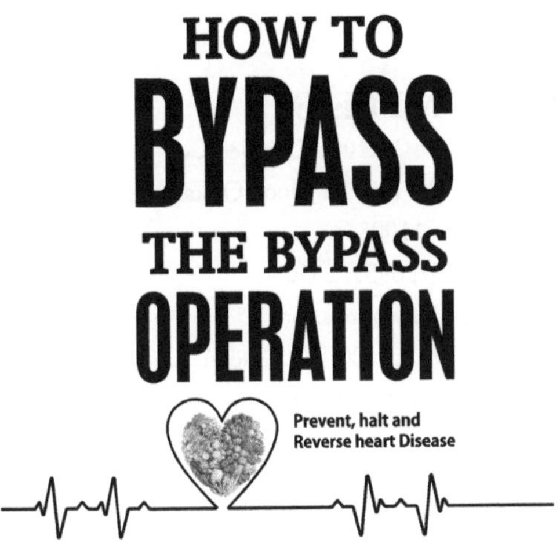

DR. SURESH BHAGIA

Worldwide Publishing by
Pendown Press

PENDOWN PRESS
An ISO 9001 & ISO 14001 Certified Co.,
Regd. Office: 2525/193, 1st Floor, Onkar Nagar-A,
Tri Nagar, Delhi-110035
Ph.: 09350849407, 09312235086
E-mail: info@pendownpress.com
Branch Office: 1A/2A, 20, Hari Sadan, Ansari Road,
Daryaganj, New Delhi-110002
Ph.: 011-45794768
Website: PendownPress.com

First Edition: 2023

ISBN: 978-93-5554-494-0

Layout and Cover Designed by Pendown Graphics Team
Printed and Bound in India by Thomson Press India Ltd.

HOW TO BYPASS THE BYPASS OPERATION

Prevent, halt and Reverse heart Disease

PRAISE
for the book

Mr. JB

"**Mr. JB** from the USA was suffering from coronary artery disease. He has been on this plant based whole food diet and was able to avoid the coronary bypass operation by following the specific diet in DiME program. He is very grateful for our service and the extra value given to him during his interactions with us."

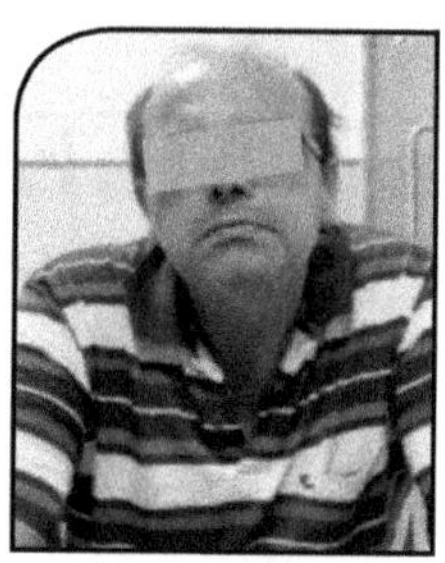

Mr. Nilesh H

"**Mr. Nilesh Hadani** was suffering from diabetes for a decade. He recently developed extensive coronary artery disease with low ejection fraction. He had shortness of breath on walking even a few feet. He started following our diet system and got very good results. His diabetes has been controlled and he has been off the diabetes medications after one month of joining our program. His wife is very satisfied and claims that they would blindly trust our team with anything and everything we do for them. Please search **Mr. NH CAD reversal Dr. SB** link @YouTube video testimonial."

ECHO CARDIOGRAPHY REPORT

PATENT'S NAME: MR. NILESH THAKKAR
SEX: MALE AGE: 53 YRS

1. Dilated LV with severe LV systolic dysfunction. LVEF: 15-20 %
2. IVS, apex and anterior akinetic, Other segments are severely hypokinetic.
3. Reduced LV compliance (Grade II)..
4. Mildly dilated LA. Normal size RA and RV. Normal RV function. TAPSE: 18 mm.
5. All valves are structurally normal.
6. Mild PAH. RVSP = 37 mmHg.
7. IVS & IAS are intact.
8. 24X14 mm size KV apical clot.
9. No vegetation seen. No pericardium effusion.
10. Doppler: No AR, Mild MR, No PR, Mild TR.
11. IVC is normal in size and well collapse on inspiration.

Conclusion:

Severe LV systolic dysfunction.
RWMA +.
Mild MR, Mild TR, Mild PAH.
Large LV apical clot.

TEST REPORT

ame	NILESHBHAI THAKKAR	Reg. No.	112203723
ge/Sex	53 Years / Male Passport No.	Reg. On	06-Nov-2022 08:25 AM
ef. By		Collected On	06-Nov-2022 08:25 AM
lient Name	: SCIENTIFIC DIAGNOSTIC CENTRE : SOLA	Approved On	: 06-Nov-2022 09:23 AM
ample Type	: Heparin,Serum	Generated On	: 06-Nov-2022 10:27 AM
		Ref ID	

arameter	Result	Unit	Biological Ref. Interval
	BIOCHEMICAL INVESTIGATION		
	* HCO3 (BICARBONATE)		
HCO3 (BICARBONATE)	16.28	mmol/L	22 - 31
	VALUE RETESTED.		
	POTASSIUM		
otassium	4.79	mmol/L	SERUM : 3.5-5.1 PLASMA : 3.4-4.5
	SODIUM		
odium	141.67	mmol/L	137 - 145
	HOMOCYSTEINE ESTIMATION		
OMOCYSTEINE ZYME CYCLING METHOD	H 20.99	Micromol/L	0 - 15
	SERUM CREATININE ESTIMATION		
REATININE ffe's Buffer - Kinetic)	H 1.28	mg/dL	0.67 - 1.17
	IDMS Traceable Reference Range.		

Patient Name : Nileshbhai Thakkar
Reffered by :
Sample No. : 6278

Age/Sex : 53 Years/Male

Ref. No : 6278

Date : 05/11/2022

LIPID PROFILE

[By Fully Automated Sysmax BX - 3010]

Sample : Serum

Test	Result	Unit	Expected Values
Serum Cholesterol (CHOD POD)	: **199**	mg/dl	110.00 - 200.00
Serum Triglyceride (GPO PAP)	: **110**	mg/dl	50.00 - 150.00
S. HDL Cholesterol (PEG Direct)	: **45.3**	mg/dl	40.00 - 100.00
S. LDL Cholesterol [Calculation]	: **97.6**	mg/dl	65.00 - 100.00
S. VLDL Cholesterol [Calculation]	: **22**	mg/dl	10.00 - 30.00
Cholesterol/HDL [Calculation]	: ***4.39***		0.00 - 4.10
LDL/HDL [Calculation]	: **2.15**		0.5 - 3.0

NEW ATP III GUIDELINES MODIFICATION OF NCEP

CHOLESTEROL
Desirable: < 200
Border Line: 200 - 239

TRIGLYCERIDE
Desirable: < 150
Border Line: 150 - 199
High: 200 - 499

LDL CHOLESTEROL
Desirable: < 100
Near or above optimal: 100-129
Borderline: 130 - 159
High: 160-189

HDL CHOLESTEROL
Low risk: > 60
High risk: < 40

Mr. Vinayak B

"**Mr. Vinayak Barve** from Vadodara was suffering from diabetes and severe coronary artery disease. Coronary artery disease was diffuse in all the coronary arteries like the LAD and circumflex and right coronary arteries.

He is pleased with the progress he has achieved in laboratory reports. He is all praises for our plan. He would recommend this plan to anybody with heart disease, especially severe coronary artery blockages. He is off his anti diabetic pills now."

(Please see the YouTube video testimonial search **Mr. VB CAD reversal Dr. SB** for details)

CORONARY ANGIOGRAPHY REPORT

NAME	
AGE/SEX	60 Years/Male
DATE	17/11/2022
CATH LAB NO.	56867
REFERRED BY	
PERFORMED BY	
In-time: -1:20 pm	Out-time: -1:40 pm
CORONARY ANGIOGRAPHY ROUTE:	Right Radial.
LMCA	Distal plaque.
LAD	Proximal segment has 90% stenosis, Distal segment has 90% occlusion.
LCX	Non-dominant, 90% stenosis in mid segment, OM has 90% ostio-proximal lesion.
RCA	Dominant, Proximal segment has 70-80% lesion , distal segment has totally occlusion. Filled retrogradelly.
CONCLUSION	Recent ACS, IWMI, Moderate LV Dysfunction, Critical TVD.
ADVICE	CABG Surgery, Aggressive diet & life style modification as advised.

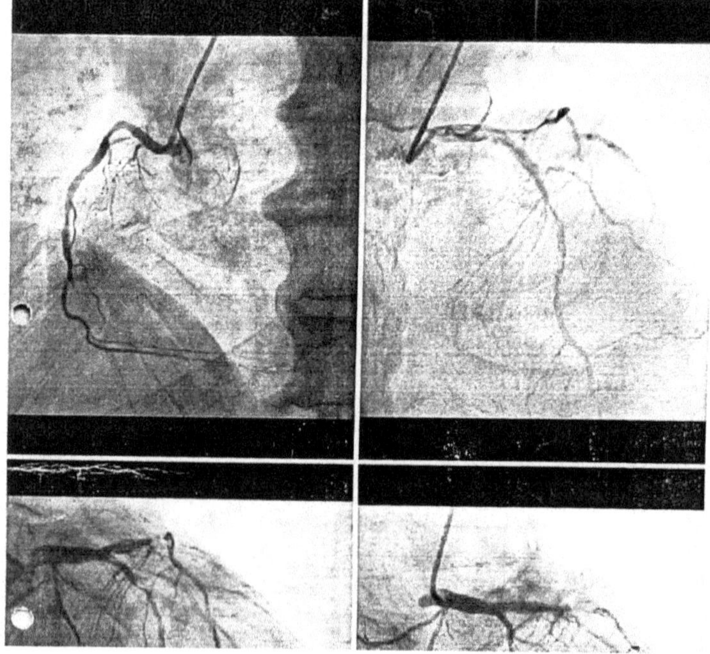

ECHO-COLOUR DOPPLER REPORT

Name: MR. VINAYAK V BARVE **Age / Sex** 56YRS/M **Date** 16-11-2022

Ref

CLINICAL C/O CHEST PAIN

SECTOR ECHOCARDIOGRAPHY :

LV show ischamic affection,
Entire anterior, mid anteroseptum, all distal segments & apex are hypokinetic
Other cardiac segments show normal excursions.
Non dilated LV with Severe LV systolic dysfunction at rest (LVEF 30-35 %)
Cardiac valves are normal in structure & excursions.
RVOT / MPA are normal. Pulmonary valve normal.
Normal sized IVC, collapsing with respiration
No e / o clot mass seen.

COLOUR FLOW , CW , PW & HAEMODYNAMIC DATA :

Grade I LV diastolic dysfunction.
Mild MR / No AR / Mild TR.
RVSP :- 30mmHg (Normal IVC)
No e/o Lt --> Rt shunt.

CONCLUSION :

- Ischaemic heart disease.
- Non dilated LV with Severe LV systolic dysfunction at rest (LVEF 30-35 %)
- Regional wall motion abnormality.
- Normal valves, Mild MR / No AR / Mild TR.No PAH
- No LV apical clot / thrombus.
- Normal sized IVC, collapsing with respiration
- No pericardial and pleural effusion noted.

Name : MR. VINAYAK BARVE
Ref. by :
Reg. Date : 07/12/2022 07:22 **Accession No. :** 0
Lab Ref No. : W298113
Age / Sex : 60 Year(s) / Male
Pt. Id :
Report Status Final

12 HRS FASTING

PLASMA GLUCOSE

Specimen : **Coll.**
FLUORIDE PLASMA FASTING 07/12/2022 07:30: Lab Collection
FLUORIDE PLASMA PPBS 07/12/2022 13:11: Lab Collection

Test Parameter	Result(s)	Biological Reference Interval (Adult)	
FBS (Plasma) Fasting Plasma Glucose	**88 mg/dL**	70 - 100	(GOD-POD)
PP2 BS (Plasma) Post Prandial 2 hr Plasma Glucose	**103 mg/dL**	60 - 140	(GOD-POD)
Status Therapy	**On Tab**		
Test note	.		

Fasting blood glucose (FBS) is to be done in the morning after overnight fasting of atleast 8 hrs.
Postprandial blood glucose (PP2BS) is not recommended for diagnosis; fasting and post glucose sample is prefeable (FBS PG2BS).
For glycemic control, use of HbA1c is preferred over plasma glucose. Blood glucose can be used for monitoring by self-monitoring of blood glucose (SMBG).

Glycemia control for people with diabetes

Test	Glycemia control
Preprandial plasma glucose mg %	80 - 130
Peak Postprandial (1-2 hrs) plasma glucose mg %	< 180
Hb A 1c %	< 7
eAG mg %	< 154

Urine glucose testing is not recommended for routine care of patients with diabetes mellitus
Urine ketone measurements is not recommended for diagnose or for monitoring the course of Diabetic Ketoacidosis.
(Recommendation, Am. Diabetic Association)
Lab performs urine glucose only on specific request and in patients on SGLT2 inhibitor drugs.

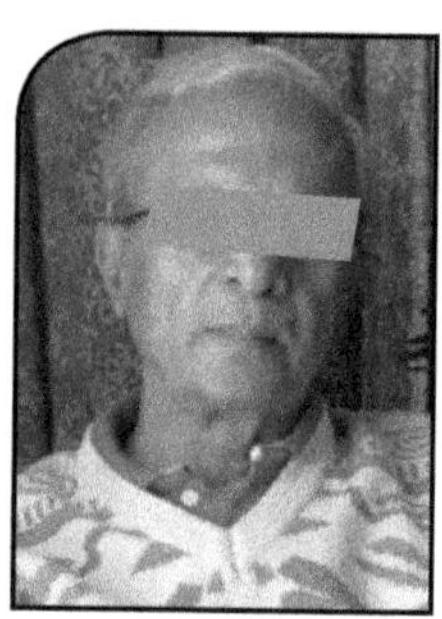

Mr. Neelam

"**Mr. Neelam** Doctor residing in the outskirts of Ahmedabad was suffering with a very low ejection fraction and severe coronary artery heart disease. He is not a doctor by profession but his surname is Doctor.

He followed a strictly vegetarian diet and improved his ejection fraction from a low EF of 15% to a moderate 45% ejection fraction.

His progress was impressive and he would like to share his benefits following this kind of a plan. Please see his video testimonial to generate faith in this kind of a program. Please search Mr. ND CAD reversal EF Dr. SB on youtube."

Mr. Shailesh K

"**Mr. Shailesh Kaka** is a gentleman from a town in Coastal Gujarat i.e. Jamnagar. We call any uncle in Gujarat as Kaka. This gentleman had a very severe coronary artery disease/ blockage in all the coronary blood vessels. The calcium score was more than 1100 CT calcium scoring system. He was extremely cautious and very disciplined and followed a raw vegan diet for 3 months. He stopped milk and also started taking water enema 2 times a day. He got amazing results in 3 months and his blockages reduced to almost 40% to 50% within a span of three months. His angiography reports have been photo copied and kept on display as evidence in this book with his courtesy. You may see other reports also which have been kept as reference material in this book. Please see our interaction with him on YouTube."

Search Mr. SK Jamnagar CAD reversal Dr. SB.

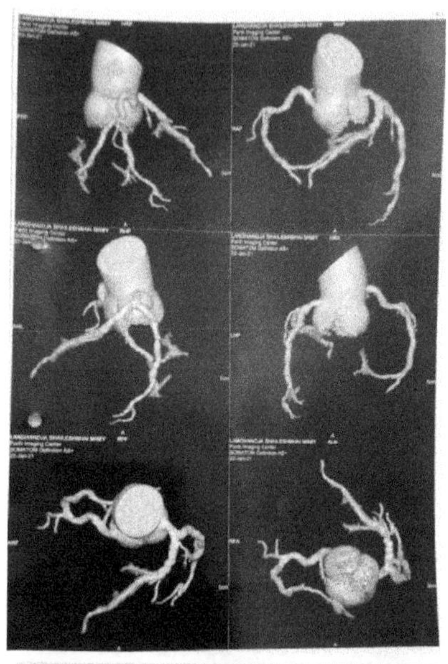

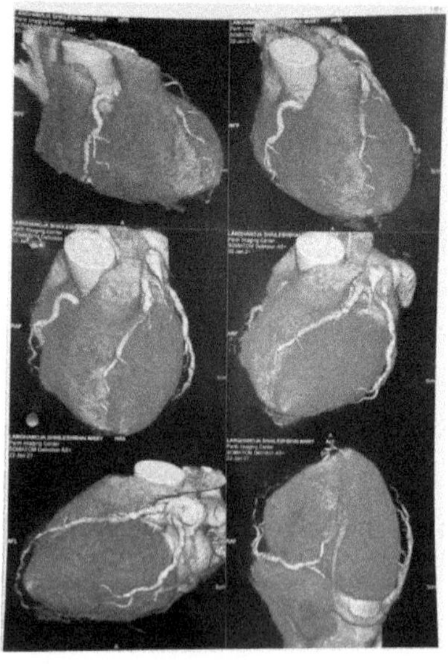

CORONARY ANGIOGRAPHY REPORT

Name	: Mr. Shaileshbhai Langhanoja
Age/Sex	: 67 Yrs/M
Date	: 28/10/2020
Cath No	: 7404
Referred By	:
Done by	:
Coronary Angiography	: DONE BY RIGHT RADIAL ROUTE.
LMCA	: Calcific, D
LAD	: Calcific, Osteal Plaque, Mid 80% Lesion (Best seen in RAO Caudal View), Diagonal 70% Lesion.
LCX	: Mid 90% Lesion, OM 70% Lesion.
RCA	: Dominant, Proximal Plaque, Mid 90% Lesion, PD 90% Lesion.
CONCLUSION	: CAD, TVD, LMCA Disease, Mild LV Dysfunction, Old IWMI (TX), HTN.
ADVICE	: CABG.

Patient Name:
Age/sex: 68 Yrs. /Male
Date: 22.01.2021

CT CORONARY ANGIOGRAPHY

TECHNIQUE:- CT study of coronary arteries was performed on 128 on SLICE SCANNER.
Calcium score performed.
75cc of Non-ionic (350 mg/ml) contrast was given intravenously.
Average heart rate was 60 bpm. (56 - 72 bpm).
Medication- Betaloc 75 mg given prior to procedure.

FINDINGS:-

CALCIUM SCORE – 1161.7
Coronary Arteries-Normal in origin

Right dominant circulation

LMCA- Calcified plaque at distal LMCA extending to LAD ostium with moderate stenosis (about 50 %).
LAD-LAD is type -III.
Dense calcified short segment plaque at osteoproximal segment with mild to moderate stenosis (about 40 %). Mid segment shows short segment mixed plaque with moderate stenosis (about 60 %). Length of the involved segment is about 6.1 mm.
D1- Osteal significant stenosis.
Cx- Non dominant. Osteal calcified plaques with no evident stenosis. Mid segment shows focal mixed plaque with mild to moderate stenosis (50 - 60 %). Length of the involved segment is about 5.9 mm. Diffuse disease at mid and distal segment with no significant stenosis.
OM – Osteal soft plaque with significant stenosis (about 70 – 80 %).
RCA- There are multiple predominantly calcified plaques at proximal and mid segment. Mid segment shows mixed eccentric plaque with significant stenosis (about 70 %) with length of the involved segment about 4.7 mm.
PDA - Soft plaques at proximal aspect. **PLVB** appear normal.

ECHO CARDIO GRAPHY REPORT

ID :-3355

DATE :- 10/10/2020

NAME :-

AGE/SEX :- 67 YRS/M

REFERRED BY DR :- SELF

CLINICAL DIAGNOSIS:-

CONCLUSION :-

*SECTOR ECHOCARDIOGRAPHY

- ALL HEART CHAMBERS ARE NORMAL
- ALL VALVES ARE NORMAL
- IAS & IVS ARE INTACT
- INFERO LATERAL WALL HYPOKINESIA SEEN
- NO E/O PERICARDIAL EFFUSION SEEN
- NO E/O CLOT OR VEGETATION
- VISUAL EF IS 40 %

* DOPPLER AND HAEMODYNAMIC DATA

- NO MR / AR / TR
- NORMAL FLOW ACROSS ALL VALVES
- REDUCED LV SYSTOLIC FUNCTION

DIAGNOSIS :- INFERO LATERAL WALL HYPOKINESIA WITH MODERATE LV SYSTOLIC DYSFUNCTION.

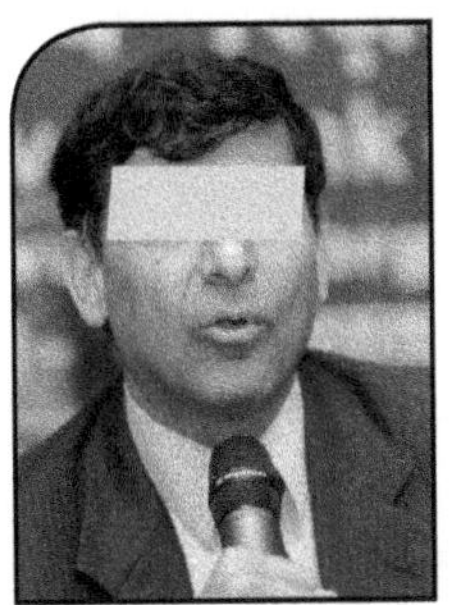

Mr. G

Mr. G, a marathon runner from Mumbai, is following the DiME program. He was recently diagnosed with blockages in the heart. His angiography report is attached. His cholesterol levels were over 220 mg. A detailed history of his dietary habits revealed that he consumed eggs for breakfast regularly and included chicken in majority of his meals. Certain social stressors were also the cause for his heart condition. We will be updating and uploading his improved reports in the next edition.

Name	:	Gender : Male	Age : 51 Years
UHID	:	Bill No :	Lab No :
Ref. by	: Self	Date : 20-Mar-2023	Time : 11:04 AM

TMT(Tread Mill/Stress Test)

Result : **Positive**

IMPRESSION

INDICATION : SCREENING FOR CAD.
PROTOCOL : BRUCE.
EX. TIME : 08.02min.
ESTD. WORKLOAD:11.50.Mets.
END POINT : TARGET HR ACHIEVED.
MAX HR ACHIEVED 162bpm (95% of THR).
MAX BP : 130/80mmHg.
SYMPTOMS : NIL.
SIGNS : NIL.
ECG CHANGES : UPSLOPING ST-T CHANGES AT PEAK EXERCISE NOTED.
ARRHYTHMIA : NIL.
CONDUCTION DISTURBANCES : NIL.

IMPRESION.
GOOD EFFORT TOLERANCE.
NORMAL HR & BP RESPONSE.
NO ANGINA , UPSLOPING ST-T CHANGES AT PEAK EXERCISE NOTED. .
STRESS TEST IS POSITIVE FOR INDUCIBLE MYOCARDIAL ISCHAEMIA.

Weight:

Race: Asian

Study Date: 20.03.2023
Test Type: --
Protocol: BRUCE

Referring Physician: --
Attending Physician:
Technician: --

Medications:
--

Medical History:
--

Reason for Exercise Test:
--

Exercise Test Summary

Phase Name	Stage Name	Time In Stage	Speed (km/h)	Grade (%)	HR (bpm)	BP (mmHg)	Comment
PRETEST	SUPINE	00:20	0.00	0.00	64	110/70	
	STANDING	00:16	0.00	0.00	63		
	HYPERV.	00:16	0.00	0.00	69		
	WARM-UP	00:34	0.30	0.00	67		
EXERCISE	STAGE 1	01:33	2.70	10.00	96	114/70	
	STAGE 2	03:00	4.00	12.00	116	120/70	
	STAGE 3	03:00	5.40	14.00	141	130/80	
	STAGE 4	00:30	6.70	16.00	162		
RECOVERY		04:03	0.00	0.00	67	120/80	

The patient exercised according to the BRUCE for 8:02 min:s, achieving a work level of Max. METS: 11.50. The resting heart rate of 74 bpm rose to a maximal heart rate of 162 bpm. This value represents 95 % of the maximal, age-predicted heart rate. The resting blood pressure of 110/70 mmHg , rose to a maximum blood pressure of 130/80 mmHg. The exercise test was stopped due to Target heart rate achieved.

Interpretation

Summary: Resting ECG: see 12SL interpretation.
Functional Capacity: normal.
HR Response to Exercise: appropriate.
BP Response to Exercise: normal resting BP - appropriate response.
Chest Pain: none.
Arrhythmias: none.
ST Changes: Upsloping ST-T changes at peak exercise.
Overall impression: STRESS TEST IS POSITIVE FOR INDUCIBLE MYOCARDIAL ISCHAEMIA..

Name of the Patient :

Age/Gender : 51 y / m

Date : 25 / 03 / 23

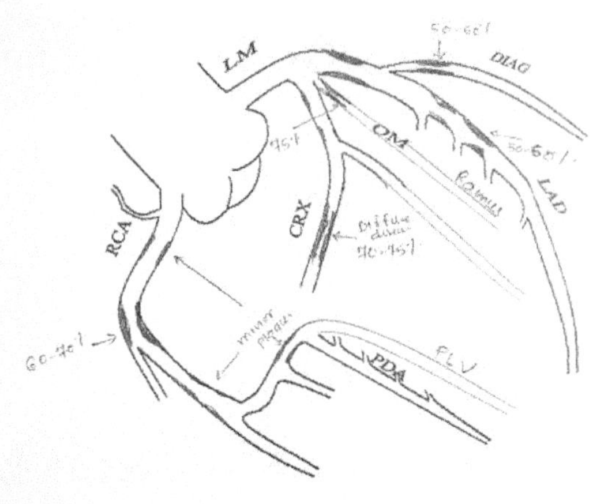

COMMENTS : Suggest – Catheter angiography

Date: 25-Mar-2023

Age : 51 Sex MALE

Name :

MULTISLICE CT CORONARY ANGIOGRAPHY

ECG gated multislice CT coronary angiography was performed with sub millimeter axial sections acquired during bolus administration of IV contrast material. This was preceded by a plain scan of the coronary arteries for calcium scoring.

Calcium score : 220, 80th percentile correlated with the age and sex of the patient.

Left main coronary artery : Appears normal.

Left anterior descending artery : Exhibits few mixed plaques in mid segment causing 50-60% luminal stenosis. Few minor soft plaques are seen in proximal segment. Rest of LAD appears normal. D1 exhibits mixed plaques in proximal segment causing approx. 50-60% luminal stenosis. D2 appears normal.

Ramus : Exhibits mixed plaques in proximal segment causing 75% luminal stenosis. Ramus measures 2.2 mm in diameter.

Circumflex : Exhibits severe diffuse disease in mid - distal segment causing 70-75% luminal stenosis. Gives rise to OM branches which also appear normal.

Right coronary artery : Dominant vessel, exhibits mixed plaques in proximal genu causing 60-70% luminal stenosis. Few minor plaques are seen in proximal, mid and distal segments. Gives rise to PDA and PLV branches which also appear normal.

Suggest : Catheter angiography if clinically indicated.

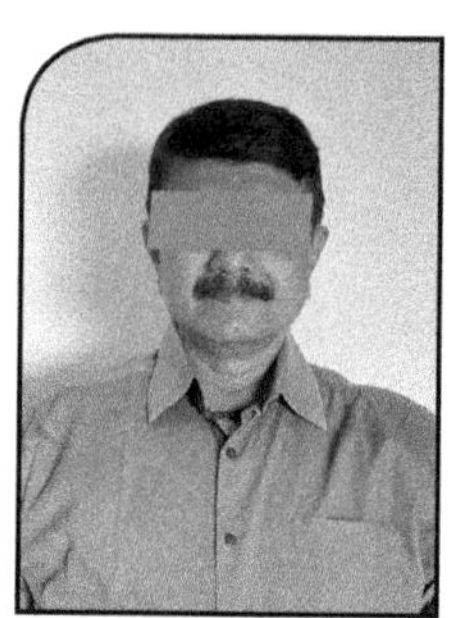

Mr. Atish

Mr. Atish, a resident of Ahmedabad, Gujarat, India, had his coronary artery disease diagnosed last year, early in 2022. His lifestyle was erratic. His calcium score on coronary CT angiography was more than 2000.. His heart blockages showed a narrowing of more than 80%. He was determined to avoid coronary bypass surgery. So, he followed a disciplined lifestyle. He changed his sleeping time from 11:30 P.M. to 10 P.M. He is also going for early morning walks, doing Pranyama and meditation. He is fully vegetarian now. He does not consume any added oil, salt or sugar. He has shared his series of echocardiography reports for the inspiration and motivation of all the readers with low ejection fraction and coronary artery disease. He has been asymptomatic from heart disease for a year now.

2D ECHO-CARDIOGRAPHY WITH COLOUR DOPPLER

	Visit# 17-Jan-2022 3:34 PM	
Patient:	- 56y Male	Ref. By: Dr

Echo Date & Time: 17-Jan-2022 15:34

- **DCMP**

- **Dilated LV**, Normal sized LA, RA, RV.
- **Severe LV Systolic Dysfunction, LVEF: 20%.**
- **Severe global LV hypokinesia.**
- Grade III diastolic dysfunction.
- All cardiac valves are structurally normal.
- Mild-to-Moderate MR, Mild TR, Trivial PR, No AR.
- Mild PAH, RVSP: 35 mm Hg.
- Normal RV Systolic function.
- IAS/IVS: Intact.
- No clot/vegetation/pericardial effusion

2D ECHO-CARDIOGRAPHY WITH COLOUR DOPPLER

	Visit# 25-Feb-2022 3:52 PM	
Patient	- 56y Male	

Echo Date & Time. 25-Feb-2022 15:52

- **DCMP**

- **Dilated LV**, Normal sized LA, RA, RV.
- **Severe LV Systolic Dysfunction, LVEF: 25%.**
- **Severe global LV hypokinesia.**
- Grade-I diastolic dysfunction.
- All cardiac valves are structurally normal
- Grade II MR, Mild TR, Trivial PR, No AR.
- No PAH, RVSP: 30 mm Hg.
- Normal RV Systolic function.
- IAS/IVS: Intact.
- No clot/vegetation/pericardial effusion

2D ECHO-CARDIOGRAPHY WITH COLOUR DOPPLER

	[illegible]t# 07-Apr-2022 3:09 PM	
Patient:	[illegible]y Male	Ref. By: D

Echo Date & Time: 07-Apr-2022 15:[illegible]

- DCMP

- **Dilated LV,** Normal sized LA, RA, RV
- **Moderate LV Systolic Dysfunction, LVEF: 30-35%.**
- **Global LV hypokinesia.**
- Stage-I diastolic dysfunction.
- All cardiac valves are structurally normal
- Mild MR, Mild TR, Trivial PR, No AR
- No PAH, RVSP: 28 mm Hg
- Normal RV Systolic function.
- IAS/IVS: Intact.
- No clot/vegetation/pericardial effusion

Date

2D ECHO-CARDIOGRAPHY WITH COLOUR DOPPLER

	Visit# 05-Aug-2022 3:31 PM	
Patient:	--56y Male	Ref. By:

Echo Date & Time: 05-Aug-2022 15:45

- **Dilated LV,** Normal sized LA, RA, RV.
- **Moderate LV Systolic Dysfunction, LVEF: 40%.**
- **Mild global LV hypokinesia.**
- Grade I diastolic dysfunction.
- All cardiac valves are structurally normal.
- Mild MR, Mild TR, Trivial PR, No AR.
- No PAH, RVSP: 25 mm Hg.
- Normal RV Systolic function.
- IAS/IVS: Intact.
- No clot/vegetation/pericardial effusion

Date :

2D ECHO-CARDIOGRAPHY WITH COLOUR DOPPLER

	Visit# 30-Mar-2023 1:21 PM	
Patient: A	,-57y Male	Ref. By:

Echo Date & Time: 30 Mar 2023 14:25

- **Dilated LV**, Normal LA size.
- **Mild LV Systolic Dysfunction, LVEF: 45%.**
- **Mild global LV hypokinesia.**
- Stage-I diastolic dysfunction.
- All cardiac valves are structurally normal.
- Mild MR, Mild TR, Trivial PR, No AR.
- No PAH, RVSP: 22 mm Hg.
- Normal RA, RV size and function.
- IAS/IVS: Intact.
- No clot/vegetation/pericardial effusion.

Illustration

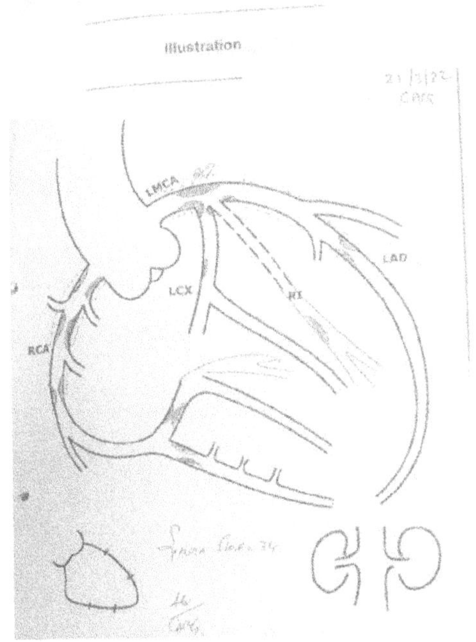

Dedicated

To All Readers

The author seeks the readers' blessings after they benefit from implementation of DiME.

The author seeks forgiveness for any unintentional errors and for the original hazy images (as received) or subtle mistakes.

Table of Contents...

The Key Essence of This Book

A disciplined lifestyle can work wonders for your heart. Heart disease and other chronic lifestyle diseases can be controlled and even reversed by following these simple steps (as mentioned in this book later). The three essential components of this lifestyle or process are detailed here, so that readers can find it easy to implement and use this book as a mentor or coach by using the 'To-Do daily diary' provided on the last page(s).

Acknowledgements

I am grateful to

1. My father, Thakurdas and my mother, Dropti who made sure that I became a good humanitarian doctor.
2. My wife, ENT surgeon, Dr. Vinita for her constructive criticism and lengthy medical discussions.
3. My daughter Reema, who inspired me to do yoga; and my son Sunny, who motivated me rapidly towards digitalization and advanced technology.
4. My teachers, firstly, Dr. Denton Cooley for mentoring me physically at Texas Heart Institute on how to perform coronary bypass surgery efficiently, and secondly, Dr. Caldwell Esselstyn Jr. of Cleveland Clinic, Ohio, for motivating me to promote the concept of "bypassing the bypass operation naturally.", from his personal experience
5. My brother, Umesh, an orthopedic surgeon in USA, for furtively encouraging me to become an entrepreneur incorporating social duties.
6. My publisher, Shri Dinesh Verma ji, for editing and printing this book in a record time.

7. Last but not the least, all my patients, surgical and non-surgical, for submitting their personal data like ECG, Echocardiography and coronary angiography reports for publication and putting their entire trust in my team of doctors and paramedic staff wholeheartedly.

Introduction

Dr. Suresh Bhagia
International Cardiothoracic Surgeon

Coronary artery disease has been a devastating illness since the last two decades as the developing nations became more affluent. Coronary artery disease can be rapidly lethal and has been labeled as a "widow-maker" disease.

Although women are not immune from coronary blockages, men are affected more by this ailment in terms of both quantity and quality of the disease process.

The month of March 2023, Indian newspapers and social media like Instagram and Twitter mentioned the heart attack suffered by the 1994 Miss Universe pageant holder (first Indian woman winner), Ms. Sushmita Sen. Although, in her mid forties, and Sushmita appears physically fit, Sushmita's heart had a 95% blockage in her left main coronary artery. It is important to note that a non-vegetarian dietary lifestyle definitely promotes coronary artery blockages. Compare and contrast this with the strict vegetarian diet and disciplined daily yoga lifestyle of the fit Bollywood superstar Rekha or even the superfit vegan Bollywood action-comedy superstar Akshay Kumar.

See the photo of Rekha and Akshay Kumar with Dr. SB.

Rekha, Akshay Kumar Houston January, 1999

The author, Dr. Suresh Bhagia, an international cardiothoracic surgeon is based in Ahmedabad, Gujarat, India.

I am privileged to have interacted and worked with several pioneering international heart surgeons of impeccable reputation in this field of cardiac sciences.

To name a few, I am listing some of them below:

1. Dr. Denton Cooley (my mentor) at Texas Heart Institute, USA.

Introduction

May 3, 2001

To Whom It May Concern:

This letter will confirm that Dr. Suresh T. Bhagia began a fellowship at the Texas Heart Institute in cardiovascular surgery on May 14, 1999 which will continue through May 14, 2001. Dr. Bhagia has remained in good standing throughout his fellowship.

Dr. Bhagia earned his medical degree in 1986 from Baroda Medical College in Baroda, India. He successfully completed post-doctoral training in general and cardiothoracic surgery there from 1986-1992. From 1993 – 1995, he obtained cardiothoracic surgical training in the U.K. at several well regarded institutions. In 1995 he served an internship at the Hospital of St. Raphael, New Haven, CT followed by postdoctoral training in anesthesiology at the University Medical Center of Stony Brook, NY before joining our service in Houston.

During his two years with our service, he has participated in a large volume and variety of cardiac, vascular and thoracic surgical procedures. Moreover, he has had an active role in the pre and postoperative care of CV patients, and on call responsibilities in the ICUs and floors. He is a mature, experienced and capable surgeon with potential to become a strong asset to his country and his profession.

Yours truly,

Denton A. Cooley

Denton A. Cooley, MD

DAC/dh

2. Dr. Michael DeBakey at Methodist Hospital, Texas, USA.

3. Professor Sir Magdi Yacoub in Harefield Hospital, UK.

With professor Dr Magdi Yacoub at Harefield in March 1999

4. John Reardon in Wellington, New Zealand

5. Dr. M. R. Girinath at Apollo Hospital, Chennai.

6. Dr. K M Cherian in Chennai, India.
7. Dr. Gunness at SSR National Hospital, Mauritius
8. Dr. Carlos Duran of Montana, USA.

9. Dr. Alain Carpentier of Paris, France (Renowned heart valve pioneering surgeon)

10. Prof. Albert Starr of Oregon, USA - maker of Starr-Edwards ball in cage heart valve

11. Professor Sir Brian Barratt- Boyes of Greenlane Hospital, NZ

And many others...

I was fortunate to get the wide exposure and profound experience necessary to gain expertise in cardiothoracic surgery.

I have presented research papers at several International conferences and meetings held in different countries such as Japan, Germany, Slovenia, Austria, Thailand, Uganda, Mauritius, etc. I have debated on topics such as Coronary artery disease, Coronary-cameral fistula, Mitral valve repair, using left anterior small thoracotomy or LAST approach for mitral valve disease and redo complex cardiac surgery.

This book is a professional treatise for the layman. When someone wants to do some good for the universe in a genuine manner, the whole universe conspires to get it done. This held true in my case before writing this book.

Dr. Christiaan Barnard believed that one could help 150 million people by preventive medicine instead of doing 150 heart transplants. I am following and living that principle.

Professor Magdi Yacoub prayed, "God give me a thousand hands so that I can make the world free of heart disease by performing multiple operations so as to make the community free of heart ailments." Sathya Sai Baba quotes, 'What could be better than preventing disease instead of doing surgery whenever possible. Love all, serve all."

You are invited
To partake in a feast for the senses and the palate

21st October at 7.30 pm

A Breathtaking Mega cultural show by
The largest cultural society of Asia
Mr Krishnamoorthy's 'Soorya'
(Program Overleaf)

Followed by a Banquet showcasing cuisine from various
States of India at 8.30 pm

22nd October at 7.00 pm

Alto Saxophone Recital by
Dr. Suresh Bhagia, Cardiac Surgeon,
Bhagia Heart Foundation, Gujarat

Songs of Hope with an Angel's Heart by
Reena R., 'Light A Life', Bangalore

A scintillating classical dance performance by
Padma Bhushan Alarmel Valli

(Program Overleaf)

Followed by a Gala Dinner of International flavor at 8.30 pm

Venue: Convention Centre, CTC

20th WORLD CONGRESS
World Society of
Cardio Thoracic Surgeons

&

6th GLOBAL FORUM
Humanitarian Medicine in
Cardiology & Cardiac Surgery

It is with great pleasure and pride
that we invite you to the Inauguration of the
20th World Congress of World Society
of Cardio Thoracic Surgeons
&
6th Global Forum on Humanitarian Medicine
on 20th October, 2010
at the Convention Centre of Chennai Trade Centre
4pm to 7pm

Dress Code: Formal

Once Sathya Sai Baba asked a famous heart surgeon in South India, "What does progress mean to you in your case?" The doctor replied that doing maximum number of heart surgeries and high bed occupancy in the hospital would be called progressive. So, Sathya Sai Baba told him that this was a wrong notion. Progress should reduce the amount of heart disease, and not increase the number of heart operations in your hospital. An increase in the number of diseases is not progress rather it is regression.

I have been fortunate to have two (contrasting) influential mentors in my life. The first mentor is Dr. Denton Cooley and the second mentor is Dr Caldwell Esselstyn Jr.

Meanwhile, Dr. Rene Favaloro, who is the father of coronary bypass surgery, was a temporary room partner as well as locker sharing partner of my current nutrition knowledge mentor Dr. Caldwell Esselstyn Jr. at Cleveland Clinic, Ohio. Dr. Rene Favaloro was a friend and contemporary of my surgical mentor Dr. Denton Cooley as well. So, I can humbly and paradoxically say that I have 2 mentors; one for preventing heart disease (bypassing the bypass operation) and one for performing coronary bypass surgery. Interestingly, I could use the training and knowledge acquired from both of them in combination for the benefit of my patients.

Basically, this book aims to make the reader free from cardiac symptoms. Also, your test reports after implementing the DiME guidelines will reveal near-normal results so that no intervention or instrumentation would be planned by any sane doctor after seeing those standard reports.

A remarkable story about numbers...

I recall my first week in the UK, which was more than two decades ago. It was my first posting as a senior house officer at Castle Hill Hospital, Hull, England, UK. I got a call from the nursing staff around midnight that the urine output in a post-operative patient after coronary Bypass surgery had dropped to 20 ml per hour. I rushed from my living quarters in the nearby hospital campus to the surgical recovery ward where I examined and discussed the case. We decided to administer an intravenous bottle of normal saline to this patient to increase the urine output. In one hour, the patient started having a urine output of 80 ml per hour and then I went back to sleep at the doctor's accommodation.

Then the next morning at 9:00 a.m. Mr. Michael Cowen, then consultant cardiothoracic surgeon, came to the surgical ward for his Consultant grand rounds. He made a comment that the Asian doctors work extremely hard. Indian doctors are available to work even during odd hours and are saving the lives of UK patients.

Then He asked me,"What was the urine output before you started the intravenous bottle in the postoperative patient"? I replied elaborately, "It was 20 ml per hour and I wanted to reach a target of about 50 to 60 ml per hour as the weight of the patient was 85 kg."

He then asked me about my sleeping and wake-up times.

I mentioned that I sleep around 11 PM and wake up around 6 AM. So, Mr. Michael asked me, "what is your urine output from 11 PM to 6 AM?" I promptly answered, "I do not get up in the night and that the urine output is zero."

Mr. Cowen quipped that maybe one can pass a catheter in my bladder and monitor the urine output and make sure it is 50 ml per hour. The medical staff around me had a hearty laugh.

He then advised me to always treat and monitor the patient clinically and correlate the clinical findings with laboratory reports and other tests. He added that I should not just treat figures or numbers from the laboratory. But treat the patient as a whole.

I learned the lesson of my life.

Since then, I have never treated only test reports or laboratory numbers in the surgical ward or even in an Intensive Care Unit. Sometimes, ICU doctors are trained to over treat

the patients based on their readings of numbers. This was clearly demonstrated during the Corona era. Some patients with oxygen saturation of 50% to 60% emerged hale and hearty. Others who had an oxygen saturation of 90% succumbed. Some persons who have a blood sugar of 200 may be due to fear and anxiety and such a patient is not to be labeled as a diabetic and should not be treated with insulin or antidiabetic agents. Treat the patient as a whole!

Chapter 1

Who Am I?

Hello Readers!

I am Dr. Suresh Bhagia. I am a physician by profession, who also knows how to operate or perform surgery.

I consider myself a simple human being first, then qualitatively a doctor and then specifically a heart surgeon. I am at that stage in my life when I know when not to operate and how to save a person's life without surgery whenever possible.

Since my medical college days, it was my dream to help the poverty- stricken masses, especially those coming from the surrounding villages in Gujarat and western parts of India.

I still remember secretly giving money to some of my patients since they did not have the return trip bus fare after their visit to the Shri Sayajirao General Hospital in Baroda, Gujarat, India.

Since my charitable instincts were dominant, I started performing free heart surgeries for my under-priviledged

patients since 2007. During that time, my personal fees would be zero and the cost of the disposable items and medicines would be borne by my friends, donors, or patrons.

Our surgical team has a 99% success rate in treating varicose veins and spider veins using lasers. Varicose vein laser Ablation or surgery is performed cosmetically at our center.

Moreover, We have an overall success rate well over 95% in Open heart surgery, including heart valve surgery and coronary bypass surgery.

With great pride and modesty too, I humbly declare that I am the only (first and last) heart surgeon from India to have been awarded an academic prize by the former President of India, Prof. Dr. APJ Abdul Kalam.

I received the Sadasivam Gold medal in Cardiovascular surgery for securing the highest marks in India in September,

2003. Also, I am the only heart surgeon from Gujarat, Western India to be mentored by Dr. Denton Cooley, the legendary cardiac surgeon of the USA.

I was his pet trainee in the millennium year 2000. He mentioned this fact in his keynote address in the IACTS Golden Jubilee conference held in New Delhi in 2004. See exhibit copy iacts.

Cardiovascular and thoracic surgery in India

Denton A. Cooley, M.D.

On the 50th anniversary of the Indian Association of Cardiovascular and Thoracic Surgeons (IACTS), I offer my most sincere congratulations. This milestone is indeed a cause for celebration. Over the past half century, India has emerged as a leader in cardiovascular and thoracic surgery. It now ranks fourth worldwide in the number of heart operations performed (50,000 annually), with an average success rate of 98.5%. Recent years have seen the establishment of numerous world-class Indian heart centers, including the Apollo Heart Hospitals, the Escorts Heart Institute and Research Centre, the Institute of Cardiovascular Diseases (Chennai), and the Heart Hospital (Calcutta), among others. These centers are staffed with superb physicians, many of whom received their training in the United States. India also has a number of excellent medical schools and research centers. Over the years, the quality of diagnosis and surgery has risen steadily, and new technological developments have become increasingly available.

Eminent pioneers in the history of Indian cardiovascular and thoracic treatment include Dr. N. Gopinath, the "father of Indian heart surgery," who performed the first open heart operation in India in 1962; Dr. Profulla Kumar Sen, who did the first cardiac transplant in India (the sixth such transplant in the world); Professor Soma Raju, who did the first angioplasty; Dr. Naresh Trehan, who performed the first robotic operation; and Dr. B. K. Goyal, who established the first intensive care unit and mobile coronary care unit. At Bangalore Hospital, Dr. Devi Prasad Shetty has performed heart operations on 17,000 of India's poorest patients, often without charging them. These pioneers, and others too numerous to mention here, have my deepest admiration and respect.

Throughout my career, I have had the pleasure of working closely with many Indian surgeons, cardiologists, nurses, technicians, and other health care workers. I met some of these individuals at various lectures and symposiums to which I was invited in India, beginning in the 1960s. During the early years of open heart surgery, I was frequently asked to demonstrate new techniques at hospitals in Bombay, New Delhi, and other Indian cities. These educational events were extremely well attended, and I was impressed by the interest and enthusiasm of the participants.

At the Texas Heart Institute (THI), in Houston, a number of Indian surgeons have trained under my direction and later returned home to become leading heart specialists in their own right. One early visitor to our clinic who adopted some of our techniques was Dr. G.B. Parulkar, who was instrumental in developing cardiovascular surgery in Bombay. Among THI's former surgical trainees are Drs. Suresh Bhagia, Amit Chandra, David Cheeran, Eugene Fernandes, Sudhir Kelkar, Satish Kini, Sandeep Singh, Sarin Sunil, and Panangipalli Venugopal.

In addition, I have had the privilege of working closely with various Indian physicians on the staff of THI. These individuals currently include Drs. Virendra Mathur and Surendra K. Jain, two outstanding cardiologists.

Ever since THI's founding in 1962, we have had numerous patients from India, including several dignitaries and government officials and one president of your country. In recent years, referral of patients from India and other non-Western countries has decreased, not only for economic and political reasons, but also because these countries now have their own excellent facilities and physicians. In fact, India is attracting heart patients from other Asian countries and even from Europe because treatment in India is quicker and less expensive. In July 2003, worldwide attention was focused on Noor Fatima Nadeem, a 2-year-old Pakistani girl, who underwent successful repair of a congenital heart anomaly at Narayana Hrudayalaya Heart Center in Bangalore. This child, who was treated for free, came

Address for correspondence:
Denton A. Cooley, M.D.
Texas Heart Institute
P.O. Box 20345
Houston, TX 77225-0345
Tel: 832-355-4932
Fax: 832-355-3424
E-mail: dcooley@heart.thi.tmc.edu

IJTCVS
2004; 20: S04-S05

Cooley S5
Cardiovascular and thoracic surgery in India

to symbolize peace efforts between India and Pakistan. The Indian government later offered to treat 20 other Pakistani children under a similar arrangement. Unfortunately, both at home and abroad, Indians have an unusually high prevalence of coronary artery disease (11% in 2001), which occurs at a younger age than in Western countries. This excess risk is not explained by conventional risk factors alone. In addition, rheumatic heart disease, which is rarely seen any more in the West, continues to take a heavy toll among Indian young people. Currently, at least 2.5 million Indians per year need heart surgery. By the year 2020, India is expected to have the largest cardiovascular disease burden in the world. Therefore, your country provides a tremendous opportunity for cardiovascular and thoracic specialists.

India has already made enormous progress in preventing and treating tuberculosis, another disease that is much less common in the West. In 1993, through government and community cooperation, India created the second largest tuberculosis program of its kind, which now achieves a cure rate of more than 80%. This remarkable success shows the extent to which well designed public health measures can improve the well being of large populations. It also sets the standard for future programs directed against heart disease, stroke, lung cancer, and other widespread scourges.

In closing, I admire and appreciate the progress India has made in the diagnosis and treatment of cardiovascular and thoracic diseases during the past half century. To all my Indian trainees, colleagues, friends, and former patients, I send my very best wishes on this golden anniversary.

Indeed, I am thankful to our former CM of Gujarat and current Prime Minister of India, Shri Narendra Modi. He started the MA card scheme in 2012 and then the PM-JAY (Pradhan Mantri Jan Arogya Yojana) Ayushmann Bharat scheme in 2018 for Indian citizens whereby the poor patients could get their heart surgery done free of cost anywhere in India. It slowed down my charitable activities since the PM-JAY scheme is applicable at Pan India level. I had been doing similar good karma at the local level all alone and covertly since 2008.

World famous heart surgeon, Dr. Christiaan Barnard, performed his first heart transplant surgery in South Africa.

In his fourth decade, he was asked in an interview about his Surgical career: "Sir, what is your single regret?" Dr. Barnard promptly said, "I have saved the lives of 150 people by heart transplants. If I had focused on preventive medicine earlier, I "might have saved 150 million."

I have imbibed these words from my idol (Dr Barnard) with whom I had interacted virtually in the Missoula, Montana

Meet of the Pioneers of Cardiac Surgery, which was held on August 8, 2000. After seeking inspiration from him, I have also decided to balance the ratio of preventive medicine vs. open heart surgery. I have saved about 12,000 lives with cardiothoracic surgery in thirty long years and over 10,500 lives in just three short years since Covid 2020 with nutritional and lifestyle changes in heart patients.

Friends, I am at that stage of my life where I do not work for money, but money works for me. I use money as a medium of exchange like a barter system. My patients are completely happy and always bless me with their honest and pure feelings.

The next chapter will inspire you to continue reading further. It mentions the reason "why" I wrote this novel guide and why you should read this book!

Chapter 2

Why Did I Write This Book?

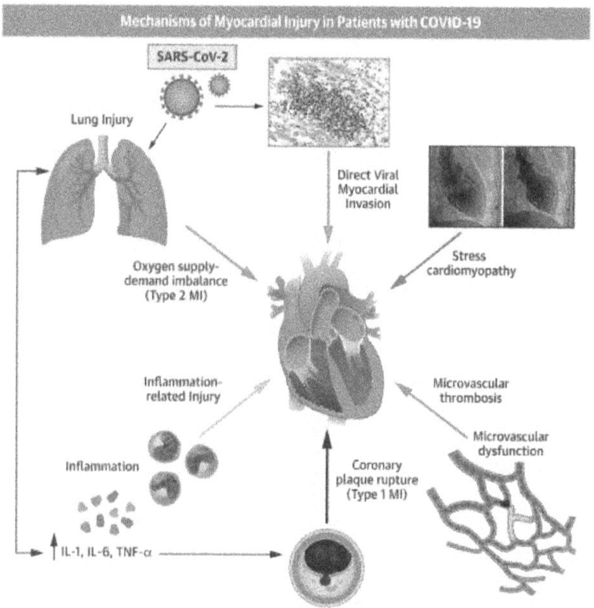

Giustino, G. et al. J Am Coll Cardiol-2020; 76(17):2011-23.

The Covid-19 times! How can anyone forget? The coronavirus era = the Covid-19 breakout worldwide, intensifying from March 2020 in India with the imposition of lockdown and curfew by our honorable Prime Minister Shri Narendra Modi, changed the lives of many people forever.

During this period and ever since I noticed that the patients were suffering more with their illnesses like diabetic foot, gangrene of the foot and heart attacks due to the thrombotic and clotting propensity of this deadly coronavirus.

Patients with coronary artery disease and coronary blockages in their heart were unable to reach the hospital due to the curfew/lockdown imposed by the law of the land or government policy. Some patients chose not to come to hospitals for their treatment. When questioned further, they told me about their fear that they would get infected in the hospital with a super added Corona virus disease.

Coronavirus was notoriously more unforgiving in people with pre-existing diseases such as diabetes, obesity, heart disease or other chronic lifestyle ailments.

These events inspired the humanitarian doctor spirit in me to think about the entire subject of coronary disease and Corona from a different and wider perspective. This made me question myself - How can I help these patients with heart blockages without doing any intervention either by some virtual means or by providing consultation on call or virtual Zoom meeting or via audio-visual presentation?

Many patients having heart disease are anyway afraid of going under the knife. While there are several elderly individuals who have limited body reserves. Moreover, in certain situations the patient's relatives feel that a heart operation might not be well tolerated by this senior citizen. In view of this predicament, I sought alternatives whereby the patient gets the treatment plus cure and stays in a safe zone without intervention.

Why should you choose to read this book?

There are several reasons why you should choose to read this book. They are listed below:

1. This can help you halt and reverse your heart disease and other chronic lifestyle diseases. The information provided in this book will even help you reverse aging in a natural way without any side effects.

2. It has a flow chart (diary and PDF style pages) at the end of the book which can be easily used by any reader. The reader can start following and implementing this plan on a daily basis and see the results themselves. Initially, You may get the basic benchmark blood tests, laboratory tests and radiological tests done as recommended. Thereafter, one can implement the plan and get the lab tests done again to see the improved changes as well as symptomatic relief obtained after a few weeks.

3. This book is scientific and based on evidence. Initially, We tried our DiME program on different patients. We have analyzed and mapped their progress. We have included proofs and evidence pertaining to actual patients for the trust of our readers. We have also provided references and reports of patients before and after following the DiME program.

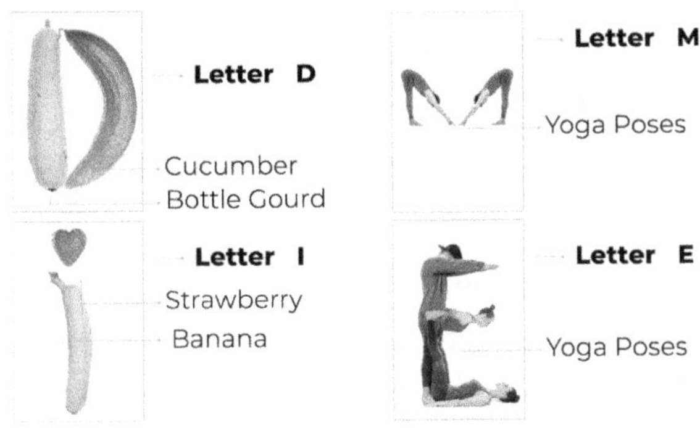

seven chakras

4. Post Covid-2 and Corona pandemic, we are conducting the DiME program via Zoom sessions. In order to encourage global reach and widespread benefits, the readers can join the session from anywhere in the world.

5. It is the best time to join this program and be a part of the community. As a member you can interact with those who had similar kinds of heart disease or problems and could overcome their chronic lifestyle diseases successfully after following the DiME program.

6. Our DiME program comes up with a concrete backup and evidence to support the results. However, there are several yoga gurus, Babas or spiritual saints (despite not being a doctor or cardiologist or cardiac surgeons or medical practitioners), who preach their ways or solutions to cure heart problems.

In case, there is an accident or an emergency, then the patient or his or her attendant can contact our team. We will provide every possible help for the patient. We are well equipped with an experienced team of experts ranging from nutrition experts, allopathic practitioners, exercise gym trainers, naturopaths, physicians, and cardiac surgeons.

It is the first time ever that this kind of a book has been written for heart disease patients by a heart surgeon who performs coronary artery bypass surgery.

I humbly request the heart patients or even a normal person (without any heart disease) to join DiME program and get its benefits. Also, I encourage the medical fraternity, especially the cardiologists and cardiac surgeons, to implement this program on their patients and pass on the benefits of the DiME program.

Moreover, I have personally benefited from the DiME program. I have followed it religiously and ensured that it is well synced with my daily routine. I have also attached my test results for your reference. My blood sugar levels were more than 300 after Covid 2020 and my diabetes got reversed successfully. I have stopped taking metformin anti-DM tablets since March 2022 (one year). Please see my photo with the CGM = the continuous glucose monitor on my left upper arm.

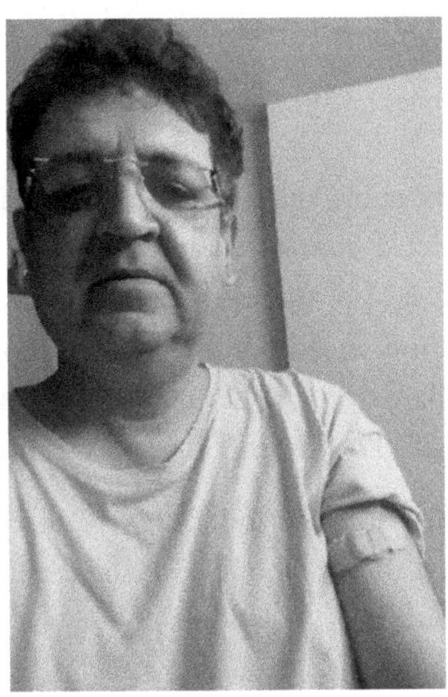

CGM of Dr. SB arm

Chapter 3

My Journey: Balance of Naturopathy and Allopathy (Science vs Spirit)

To satisfy the above quest and seek a desirable, universally acceptable answer, I contacted several doctors in the US and pan India. I have also attended several courses in nutrition, diet and meditation. I read a dozen books authored by stalwarts like Dr. Neal Barnard, Dr. Dean Ornish, Mr. Pravin Shah, Dr. John Dougall, Dr. Jason Fung and the list goes on…

I have pursued different courses in naturopathy and studied Ayurveda as well. I met Shri B. V. Chauhan, the pioneer of New Diet System or NDS.

Conference on

New Dimensions in Healthcare

July 12-16, 2007

Academy For A Better World, Gyan Sarovar

Mount Abu-307 501 (Raj.) India

Organised By: Medical Wing, GHRC & Brahma Kumaris

Friday 13th July, 2007 *Venue: Harmony Hall*

11.00am—01.00pm

CORONARY ARTERY DISEASE - PRESENT SCENARIO

Chairperson : **Dr. Ashok D. B. Vaidya, Mumbai**
Research Director,
Kasturba Health Society, Sevagram

Panelists : **Dr. Satish Gupta, Mount Abu**
Cardiologist,
Global Hospital & Research Centre

: **Dr. Suresh Bhagia, Ahmedabad**
Cardiac Surgeon,
Rajasthan Hospital

: **Dr. B. Sitaram Reddy, Hyderabad**
Consultant Cardiothoracic & Vascular Surgeon

Shri BV Chauhan of NDS at Brahma Kumaris Lotus House in Ahmedabad, Gujarat

My ongoing research and controlled experiments concluded that in order to reverse coronary blockages or heart blockages without intervention and using minimum medical therapy (like the use of some tablets which included allopathic or Ayurvedic medicines), the person should consume a balanced vegan diet. In addition to this, one must get adequate sun exposure for a minimum of 20 minutes as well as perform yoga and breathing exercises. One should also include walking or similar exercise in their fitness routine.

I have been in constant discussion with one of the leading pioneers of the reversal of coronary disease with nutrition. i.e... Dr. Caldwell Esselstyn Jr. via Zoom meetings.

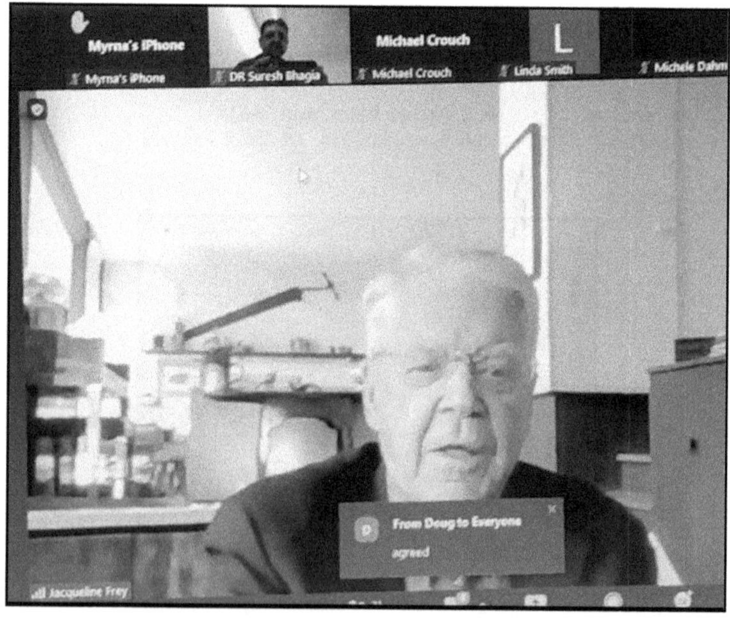

He has been a lead role model for "Forks over Knives" the famous documentary on YouTube. He has authored the New York Times Bestseller titled "Prevent and reverse heart disease" with plant based whole food nutrition.

After having seen thousands of hearts (8136 and still counting) and coronary arteries (more than 23,857 and still counting) during open heart surgery in the operation theater, I could see the calcifications and the soft and semi-solid blocks and plaques made of cholesterol and platelets physically live during the surgeries on my patients. Many times the patients had to undergo incomplete bypass or endarterectomy or unsatisfactory bypass due to their natural condition of the heart or profoundly sick or thin coronary arteries and a gross mismatch between the native coronary artery and the autologous conduit.

I extend my heartfelt gratitude to Mr. Lalit Kapoor of California, who conducted a 2 month course giving great insights about plant based nutrition and how plant based whole food diets can reverse chronic lifestyle diseases such as diabetes, thyroid disorders, hypertension as well as heart disease.

Chapter 4

What is This Book All About And What Will You Get After Reading This Book?

So, what is DiME? What will you get in this program? DiME refers to a Diet, Meditation and Exercise program that needs to be followed meticulously. The DiME program is basically for:

1. Patients who are having heart disease with a low ejection fraction or impaired pumping of the heart or

2. Patients suffering from severe and chronic coronary artery disease, which is known as diffuse heart blockages or

3. People who have undergone coronary bypass surgery or PTCA (or coronary angioplasty) or

4. People who want to remain free from heart diseases. DiME has been 100% effective for all the patients. The key reason is that first of all, there are no side effects, and it is a 100% plant based diet. The diet comprises of all the natural

micronutrients such as vitamins, minerals and macronutrients such as proteins, fats, and carbohydrates. There are no tablets or pills involved.

This diet is a very safe, time tested diet which is very effective for all the people. Though it may be difficult to follow initially, if it is pursued rightly and with 100% discipline, then the results will surely show up. In reality, it is affordable, doable and a part of the normal diet.

Following the DiME program will be a different experience.

You will get results beyond your imagination or expectation.

It will mainly work upon your high blood pressure and diabetes. It can also remove heart blockages in a few months.

Disclaimer

1. This plan would not be effective or work for those patients who have calcified coronary arteries and stiff, stubborn fibrotic blockages.
2. Patients with acute problems such as acute myocardial infarction and repeated heart attacks and angina at rest may not find the DiME program effective.
3. Patients with a failing left ventricle might need intense medical supervision and serious medical attention with SOS intervention. Hence, the DiME program may not work for them.

So, in short, by following the DiME program, one can be free from diseases, especially pertaining to the liver, kidney

and heart. The program is 100% safe and free from any side effects. However, patients might need medical supervision in those rare cases .e.g. where the persons have symptoms and need to be taken to an emergency room due to an acute myocardial infarction. These patients will need quick intervention.

However, the DiME program is ideal for patients who have had stable angina, or have been suffering from heart blockages for over six months and have not had any intervention. Also those patients who have already undergone intervention in the form of angioplasty or coronary bypass surgery will benefit as DiME prevents recurrence of their disease and eliminates the root cause.

Chapter 5

How Does The DiME Program Work?

Combining the power of Ayurveda and Naturopathy and armed with the knowledge of Pharmacology and specialized expertise in the cardiac operation theater, I started treating patients with nutrition. Diet forms 70 percent of the DiME program. This kind of conservative management reversed our patients' heart blockages via this plant- based whole food diet in some stubborn cases, as shown in the sample testimonials and images.

Having a meticulous follow-up, which showed that the patients were doing well, I felt elated and encouraged. Also, with our experienced team as a backup in case the patients required emergency intervention, this proved to be a safe and successful program. Our heart care team were always there to help the patients in case they needed intervention in the form of Bypass surgery or any other interventional procedure like angioplasty with the help of our colleagues.

Dr. Caldwell Esselstyn Jr., also shared his own studies and scientific data on the Zoom meeting and email. The documents proved that his diet, which we were following, could reverse the coronary artery disease after a few months, and many of the cases were proven symptomatically or scientifically by coronary angiography.

Even 2D echocardiography showed an improvement in the ejection fraction. Further, we could do some follow-up studies like thallium uptake scan where we could see that the hibernating myocardium became viable myocardium and, therefore the blood flow to the myocardium increased after this kind of PBWF nutrition.

Now we introduced the second key element to this therapy and that is meditation, which equals 20%. It is a straightforward kind of meditation in the sense that the patient has to sit quietly, alone or in a group, for a duration of 15 minutes or more. One must focus only on the breaths during this time.

DiME meditation is quite simple.

Count your first breath in and first breath out:

Inspiration + Expiration = One Count.

As you complete one cycle, it will be counted as round 1. This carries on and continues further.

Thus, one can count from 100 to 200 breaths (respiratory cycles) during one meditation session of 15 minutes.

During this breathing period, avoid thinking about anything. Focus only on counting your breaths.

There is no extra effort required in order to do this kind of breathing. DiME Meditation is just the flow of the breath whether fast or slow, continue breathing, observing, and counting the breaths.

Now, during inspiration, make an affirmation that health is coming in, and with every inspiration, the heart is becoming healthier.

During each expiration, think that with each breath going out, coronary disease or heart blockages are going out. Visualize and give the coronary artery blockages some form and color. Envision them (pale yellow irregular twisted rods) melting far away from you as you meditate regularly.

The third and final key element in this program is Exercise, which forms 10%.

We recommend our patients to walk daily for a minimum of 30 minutes in our DiME program. If they are not walking then they may do swimming, cycling, playing a game or similar kind of exercise.

If you are more fit and you have extra zeal then you can do aerobics or zumba as per your preference and the doctor's advice.

So we found that C, H, O or Carbon, Hydrogen and Oxygen are the main key elements in the formation of Carbohydrates, Proteins and Fats. In the same chemical structure when we add the Nitrogen element as in doing muscular exercise or weight training there is a profound shift in the benefit, and so we do recommend some kind of tension band exercises for muscle building in all age groups.

Also, most of these patients have obesity and metabolic syndrome, and we have observed that anti-gravity exercises like sitting heel lifts or arm raises can lower blood sugar levels by 30 to 50 points in 15 minutes and thus prevent a spike in sugar or insulin levels.

We have formulated the breakfast, lunch and dinner for these kinds of people and how they would benefit from these diet plans. Since, human beings live in a society, the diet plan may flip flop or may change focus as there may be a temptation.

But, that is not a major problem and one can compensate for this indulgence and cheating by doing a total dry fast or by doing Water only fast for 12 to 14 hours. Also, intermittent fasting is very important for the obese and overweight patients and definitely helps in the reversal of diabetes and hypertension without any side effects.

Readers can explore books by Dr. Jason Fung who is an authority on intermittent fasting and its benefits in chronic lifestyle diseases.

I have attached some of the testimonials given by different kinds of patients whom we have treated and the kind of satisfaction they have obtained after following our treatment plan.

We could even reverse the heart disease which was refused by doctors and patients who had refused surgery due to the high risk.

We stress the fact that DiME can help you avoid having the first heart operation and even prevent a second redo open heart surgery.

Basically, our holistic program can help those who want to avoid mechanical or external intervention or are afraid of bypass and have multiple associated diseases and risk factors.

In most cases, a successful trial can be given. In those isolated cases of not succeeding in this program our team would go for intervention and make sure that they don't suffer from the disease. Progression of disease is thus circumvented so that the complications of the disease do not endanger the life of this patient.

All the pros and cons of this therapy are explained upfront. All the options are laid open about what the patients will have to face on undergoing the surgery and problems of not doing the surgery. Also benefits of the DiME diet and complications cached by circumventing this diet plan are explained. We make sure that the patient gets the surgery done only when it is strongly indicated as a last resort.

We follow a sequential way:

1. Natural Therapy: diet and exercise

2. Allopathic or ayurvedic medicines

3. Intervention which is minimal.

   So even in the angiography, we avoid the conventional wire angiography and we advocate CT scan coronary angiography and lastly,

4. Coronary bypass surgery or PTCA.

We ensure that our patients are never forced to go for a particular form or a technique under DiME program. The patients are only informed and educated. If they need help we guide them towards the best choice by our expertise and experience in the previous cases.

Sometimes the patients are suffering with heavily calcified, diffusely diseased coronary arteries. In these cases, it may not be possible to reverse the blockages. It is best that the patient follows a diet plan to ensure that there is no dislodgement of any loose plugs or particles or atheromatous plaques which would cause further distal blockage and thereby endanger the life of such a patient.

We cannot overemphasize the fact that a loose plaque on the inner wall is more unstable and dangerous than a calcified plaque which will not dislodge. In severe coronary stenosis, even though the lumen of the vessel may be narrow and the blood flow to the heart may be less, yet it would not be life threatening because now the patient is in a chronic stable state and we can encourage him to diet and exercise. There is a collateral circulation already existing which will develop more upon progressive exercises, and thus improve the symptoms over a period of time.

After having performed thousands of such operations, I have studied everything in detail about coronary arteries during surgery, before surgery, and after surgery. I also understand how much time period it actually takes to manifest a coronary blockage, what is the rate of progression of the disease and how different coronary arteries in the operation room (surgical theater) look from the outside and inside.

How can one halt the progression of this deadly disease by controlling the factors responsible for such blockages? This is important since a cardiac surgeon like myself, does not remove the blockages during bypass surgery but just makes a bridge across the choked up blood vessel. Also if the root cause responsible for the coronary disease has not been addressed, the blockages may progress, new blockages may form and the conduits used for bypass may also get blocked by the native disease process. So, even in those selected patients where we perform coronary bypass surgery, our team ensures that the patients endeavor to follow our prescribed diet chart as much as possible.

We specialize in the treatment of reversal of heart blockages in diabetes patients and while we reverse these heart blockages, most of these patients also become non-diabetic. Their sugar (glucose) levels soon get better and under control. In fact, there is actually a permanent cure which is difficult to believe by the patients' relatives as well as their GPs and routine doctors treating these patients. Unfortunately, there is no curriculum on nutrition during our medical college education.

Fortunately, the reversal of diabetes mellitus, especially type II DM is a bonus for the patients with heart blockages upon implementing this kind of diet therapy.

However, the diet plan might fail under a few conditions:

1. The person does not follow the DiME plan strictly.
2. There are multiple factors responsible for coronary artery disease and someone who has got renal disease

and calcification or parathyroid disorders or is genetically predisposed by enzyme deficiencies for cholesterol metabolism, and liver disease.

3. If a patient is consuming either alcohol, tobacco or is consuming non-vegetarian food.
4. Idiopathic, wherein a reason cannot be found in these few cases.

Yet all the patients who follow the DiME strategy will benefit. It is 100% safe and free from any side-effects.

There are now several centers in major metropolitan cities having some kind of "reversal of heart disease" program.

We humbly declare that our program is the most cost effective and practical one as it is natural and does not require any special equipment and can be done alone or in a group with the right guidance and motivation.

There is no EECP (enhanced external counter pulsation) or Chelation therapy used by DiME for reversal of heart blockages. EECP uses expensive artificial means and pressure to open up collateral channels which we do not contest or deny. Collateral circulation can be opened up in a non-expensive scientific manner with nitric oxide rich natural foods and by gradually increasing exercise therapy.

Our program is based on the science of nutrition and the human spirit. We mention science because we do multiple laboratory tests and radiological tests and serial clinical examinations on follow up to see the progress of the disease and the improvement during the course of this kind of therapy.

Also, spirit is mentioned because this is a spiritual program since it does involve meditation like breathing techniques and some group support which is good for interaction and encouragement by the fellows who have enrolled in the program before and have seen the benefits.

Chapter 6

The story of Lord Shiva and Nandi the Bull

During ancient days, people used to seek advice and guidance from Lord Shiva to lead their lives in the best way. Lord Shiva received a delegation to help these people. Since Lord Shiva was occupied, he asked Nandi (his bull) to go and attend to the people. He told Nandi to go and tell the people, "*Din mein teen baar nahao aur ek baar khao...*" which means in Hindi that one should bathe three times in a day while they should eat only once.{ din means day, mein means in, teen means three, baar means times, nahao means bathe, aur means and, ek means one, khao means eat}.

Nandi followed the instructions of Lord Shiva and proceeded towards the delegation. He was afraid as he thought that he might forget what Lord Shiva told him to speak in the delegation. So, he kept on repeating and chanted the lines like a mantra.

He repeated loudly, "*Din main teen baar nahao aur ek baar khao...*"

He kept on chanting till he reached the delegation.

However, he didn't realize that he had muddled up the words.

Then He reached the delegation and asked the people to listen to his instructions.

So, he gathered all the people and announced, "Listen, everyone, Lord Shiva has sent me to address your delegation so that one can lead a proper life ahead." So, he announced, "*Teen bar khao aur din main ek baar nahao...*" which means that you should eat three times and bathe once in a day. He was quite content and asked the delegation to leave so that he can then return back.

People were quite delighted to get the instructions of Lord

Shiva. They reached home and started following the advice given by Lord Shiva. Similarly, other people started following in the same practice. People started eating three times a day and bathed once a day. This was a normal routine then. Slowly and gradually, there was a severe shortage of food. Soon,

Lord Shiva received another delegation who came up with this problem. They were looking for a solution. So, Lord Shiva, heard the entire problem and realized that Nandi was the real creator of this issue. Nandi had reversed his advice.

Lord Shiva was very furious. He called Nandi and yelled at him. He admonished Nandi and said, "You are the reason behind all this mess. Now, you will go and solve this problem by helping people and by growing the food that is required.."

He then curses Nandi. Thereafter, the bull is helping earthly people in growing their food. We can see that farmers have bulls that help in agriculture. They plow the fields and carry a heavy burden on their shoulders. Hence, it is the bull on earth who is paying a hefty price for the confusions done by Nandi the Bull.

Lord Shiva and the Bull Nandi

Chapter 7

All About Diet and Eating Lifestyle

Chewing the food and Clearance of heart blockages

People chewing their food properly will have less chances of obesity, diabetes, or heart blockage. Chewing food releases

Saliva. Saliva is alkaline and very protective against acidic inflammation.

There are enzymes in saliva which aid in converting the nitrates present in the plant food into nitrites. Thereafter, it gets reduced to nitric oxide which is ultimately the most powerful vasodilator on earth.

It explains the paradox we often encounter many times in our clinical practice, i.e. the clinical-pathological mismatch.

We find that the patient is eating junk food or even non-vegetarian food or pastries and has a borderline or raised cholesterol level but the coronary angiography shows normal-looking coronary arteries. That's the magical effect of chewing the food thoroughly and the sequel of nitric oxide and its vasodilator and anti inflammatory effects.

Our DiME program diet consists of Macronutrients and micronutrients:

- Macronutrients
- Carbohydrates, protein and fats

A) Carbohydrates

A balanced diet consists of macronutrients such as carbohydrates, protein, fat, which serve as sources of calories. Incorporating these macronutrients in a balanced manner can contribute to a healthy diet. To maintain, gain or lose weight, it is crucial to maintain a balance between the calories consumed and the ones burned through physical activity. Here are some tips on how to incorporate carbohydrates into your diet.

Carbohydrates have been a topic of debate in the field of nutrition, with varying opinions on their consumption. Several diets exist, including low-carbohydrate diets and high carbohydrate low-fat diets, each with different recommendations on the percentage of daily carbohydrate intake.

Carbohydrates are of two types, simple to complex.

There is a common misconception among both medical professionals and the general public that consuming higher amounts of carbohydrates can cause diabetes. While it is true that both sugar and carbohydrates can cause a spike in insulin levels and subsequent insulin resistance, this book's scope does not allow for a detailed discussion and differentiation between insulin deficiency and insulin resistance.

Not All Carbs Are Created Equal

There are three types of carbohydrates found in food: sugar, starches and fiber. The classification of carbohydrates as simple or complex depends on their chemical structure and the speed at which their sugar content is digested and absorbed.

The type of carbohydrates consumed has a significant impact on overall health, as foods that are high in simple sugars, particularly fructose, can increase triglyceride levels. High triglyceride levels, or blood fats, are a crucial indicator of metabolic health, as they may be linked to conditions such as coronary heart disease, diabetes, and fatty liver disease.

Simple carbohydrates are rapidly digested and provide an immediate burst of glucose, or energy, into the bloodstream.

This explains the surge of energy one might feel after consuming a dessert, followed by a subsequent crash when the energy is depleted. Simple sugars are primarily present in refined sugars, such as the white sugar commonly found in sugar bowls. Added sugars, including refined sugars, are sources of empty calories, lacking in essential vitamins, minerals, and fiber, and may contribute to weight gain.

However, it is essential to note that not all simple sugars are equal. Nutritious foods, such as fruits and milk, contain "naturally occurring" sugars, which differ from refined sugars.

Naturally occurring sugars are often accompanied by essential vitamins, minerals, and fiber that are beneficial to the body's needs.

Complex carbohydrates are slowly digested, resulting in a gradual and consistent release of glucose into the bloodstream.

Nevertheless, it is crucial to consider that, as with simple sugars, not all complex carbohydrate foods are equal, and some choices are better than others.

Refined grains, such as white flour and white rice, undergo processing that eliminates numerous nutrients and fiber.

Common foods containing refined grains, such as white flour, sugar, and white rice, lack essential B vitamins and other crucial nutrients, unless they are enriched. Conversely, unrefined whole grains retain many of these essential nutrients and are abundant in fiber, which promotes healthy digestive function.

Fiber also imparts a feeling of fullness, reducing the likelihood of overeating such foods. This is the reason why a bowl of oatmeal will keep you feeling fuller for a more extended period compared to consuming the same number of calories from sugary candy.

Why do I need carbohydrates?

Upon consuming carbohydrates, the body begins to break them down into simple sugars that are subsequently absorbed into the bloodstream. As the blood sugar level rises, the pancreas secretes a hormone known as insulin. Insulin is necessary for the transportation of sugar from the bloodstream to the cells, where it serves as a source of energy.

When this process goes fast — as with simple sugars like sugar-sweetened beverages and high-calorie desserts — you are more likely to feel hungry again soon.

Some foods, primarily those with high levels of simple sugars, cause blood sugar levels to rise more rapidly than others due to their carbohydrate content. The rate at which carbohydrates convert to blood glucose is evaluated on the glycemic index scale. If you are in good health, carbohydrates convert to glucose (blood sugar), which the body utilizes as a source of energy. However, if your blood glucose levels become excessively high or low, it may indicate that your body is having difficulty producing the necessary insulin to maintain good health, which could eventually lead to diabetes.

Simple carbohydrates found in processed, refined or added sugars that do not contain any nutritional value include:

1. Candy
2. Regular (non-diet) carbonated beverages, such as soda
3. Syrups esp corn syrups
4. able sugar (refined).

Complex carbohydrates, often referred to as "starchy" foods, include:

1. Legumes
2. Starchy vegetables
3. Whole-grain and fiber.

Try to obtain carbohydrates, vitamins, and other essential nutrients in their most natural form possible. For instance, choose to consume fruit instead of sugary beverages and opt for whole grains over processed flours.

When it comes to carbohydrates, it is recommended that you limit your intake of foods that are high in processed and refined simple sugars, as they provide calories but little nutrition. Instead, aim to consume more complex carbohydrates and healthy nutrients by increasing your intake of fruits and vegetables.

B) Proteins

There are many myths and misconceptions surrounding the recommended daily intake of protein and the appropriate amounts needed. Various diets, such as the Atkins and Mediterranean diets have become popular. While proteins are linked with muscle development, in reality, muscles are primarily built through tension exercises, and protein intake alone does not dictate muscle growth.

The average person requires around 0.8 grams of protein per kilogram of body weight to maintain a healthy body, which translates to approximately 50 to 70 grams for an average adult.

While non-vegetarian foods are often considered to be high in protein, there are several plant-based foods that can meet the daily protein requirements for good health. Even green leafy vegetables like spinach, kale, and fenugreek contain protein that can be substantial.

It is worth noting that vegetables and fruits also provide a good source of protein. In some cases, protein deficiency or fasting can lead to rapid weight loss and even help reverse heart disease and other chronic lifestyle diseases.

According to a study in The Lancet's E Clinical Medicine journal, diets that have fewer sulfur amino acids could be linked to a lower chance of developing heart disease.

Meats and other high-protein foods contain more sulfur amino acids. People who consume a lot of fruits and vegetables have a lower sulfur amino acid intake. These findings support the health benefits of vegan or plant-based diets.

Many high protein diets have gained popularity because they can help with weight loss. However, animal studies and some large studies in people have linked high protein diets to cardiovascular problems. Such high protein diets may directly contribute to the buildup of plaque inside arteries, which can affect cardiovascular health.

Those who consume a high fat and high protein diet have much worse atherosclerosis, compared to those who have a high-fat, low-protein diet.

A high amount of dietary protein may contribute to the formation of unstable arterial plaque.

To summarize, excessive protein intake can be harmful to cardiovascular health, and consuming 10-15% of daily calories from protein sources is sufficient. It is also advisable to avoid animal proteins and opt for vegan proteins to maintain cardiac health and to prevent or reverse heart blockages.

C) Fats

Several groups in India follow similar dietary practices such as the Sattvic movement, New Diet system, and Saaol.

Brahmakumaris group is doing a similar CAD reversal program scientifically.

However, we are the first and only group in India that comprises **cardiac surgeons**, physicians, and nutrition experts who design personalized programs based on individual patients' signs, symptoms, laboratory tests, and radiological investigations.

We modify and customize the ongoing plan with committed clinical and laboratory follow-ups to ensure optimal health outcomes.

I would like to share a real story about a patient we treated, referred to as the "50/50/50." In November 2022, we received Mrs. H.S, a 50-year-old female patient from Ahmedabad who weighed only 50 kg and measured 5 feet tall. Although her total cholesterol was 150 mg% and HDL levels were 50 mg., she was diagnosed with severe triple vessel coronary artery disease. This meant that her LAD, RCA, and Left Circumflex coronary arteries had blockages ranging from 80 to 90%. I will provide more details about her lab reports and coronary angiography in the next edition of this book.

However, for now, I want to emphasize the significance of this case.

The woman's weight and cholesterol levels were within normal range, and her HDL levels were protective. She

reported no recent family stressors or negative events. When I asked about her lunch and dinner habits, she mentioned two potentially problematic dietary factors: 1) drinking buttermilk (casein) after each meal, and 2) using groundnut oil to cook (trans fats) her meals.

Unfortunately, the patient chose not to participate in the DiME program out of fear about experiencing another futuristic heart attack. As a result, she underwent coronary bypass surgery which was performed by another cardiac surgeon a week later and was discharged from the hospital in December 2022. While the patient requested that I perform Coronary Artery Bypass Grafting, I was not convinced that CABG was necessary as she was a candidate for reversal of her heart disease through natural means. In summary, it is important to correlate a patient's clinical signs, symptoms, lifestyle, dietary habits, personal history, and family history with their investigations and reports.

On a lighter note **Cheating during the DiME** program:

Humans have a tendency to crave for a change, and variety adds flavor to our lives. Sometimes, individuals following a particular diet may deviate from it, especially during social events or weekends. In such situations, we suggest compensating for the indulgence act by doing a detox diet for the next few days.

This may include a grape juice fast, coconut water fast, or even a prolonged dry fast.

Maintaining discipline is key to achieving good health, and cheating on a diet is not recommended. However, the DiME program is so effective that even those who cheat have avoided bypass surgery by implementing 80% of the diet. This means that the disease does not progress further, even if the heart blockages may not reverse. The power of the DiME program is unmatched, making it a unique and valuable option.

Furthermore, Dr. Esselstyn's book states in chapter 5 that even moderation kills and can still lead to negative health outcomes.

- **Micronutrients - vitamins, minerals**

B complex vitamin group, such as riboflavin, thiamine, along with vitamin B6, B12 and folic acid, is beneficial for heart failure management.

Folic acid creates an improvement in endothelial dysfunction in patients suffering with several cardiovascular diseases. B complex vitamins may prevent cardiovascular diseases through the treatment of hypertriglyceridemia. Niacin, a type of vitamin B decreases total cholesterol and triglycerides. Additionally, a vitamin B complex that contains B1, B2, and B6, along with B12 and folic acid, has been shown to reduce ischemic heart disease and atherosclerosis via anti-inflammatory actions.

Combination of folic acid and vitamin B12 causes reduction of plasma homocysteine levels, which may help delay the early onset of coronary artery disease. Moreover, antioxidant vitamins, including folic acid, can reduce the risk of endothelial dysfunction in patients with coronary disease.

Vitamin C can reduce atherosclerosis in patients with ischemic heart disease by improving endothelial function and lipid profile, as well as inhibiting the oxidation of low-density lipoproteins, which may even heavy smokers. Additionally, vitamin C helps to relieve of coronary constriction and restore the coronary flow.

Vitamin A precursors like α-carotene or β-carotene, might be beneficial in various cardiovascular diseases. Vitamin A is effective in reducing both systolic and diastolic blood pressures in patients with hypertension.

Vitamin A, with its antioxidant and anti-inflammatory properties, reduces atherosclerosis in humans.

Vitamin A supplementation reduces oxidative stress levels in diabetic patients with ischemic heart disease.

The fat soluble vitamin D (calcitriol) is beneficial to patients with hypertension and heart failure by inhibiting the renin-angiotensin system and parathyroid hormone secretion, as well as acting directly on vitamin D receptors found in vascular smooth muscle cells, cardiomyocytes, and endothelial cells. increased levels of 25-hydroxyvitamin D, a precursor of calcitriol, are associated with a decreased risk of cardiovascular diseases, including myocardial infarction, aortic stenosis, and heart failure. Regular vitamin D to patients can inhibit NF-kB pathway, thereby reducing the progression of coronary artery disease and the occurrence of acute myocardial infarction.

The addition of 25-hydroxyvitamin D can reduce the progression of atherosclerosis by reducing levels of total

cholesterol, triglycerides, and low-density lipoproteins in the bloodstream, while increasing the levels of high-density lipoproteins and promoting the production of endothelial nitric oxide.

Vitamin E (α-tocopherol) is a popular nutritional supplement due to its various benefits such as antioxidant and anti-inflammatory properties, as well as its ability to boost the immune system, as shown by Pryor et al. Also, vitamin E supplements can lower blood pressure in people with essential hypertension.

Vitamin E, slows down the advancement of atherosclerosis, by reducing the severity of endothelial dysfunction.

Moreover, α-tocopherol can prevent cardiac dysfunction and damage induced by ischemia-reperfusion. This is achieved by reducing oxidative stress and inflammation. In males, the risk of coronary artery disease is reduced by the intake of Vitamin E supplements.

When there is a deficiency of vitamin K, the body produces Gla rich proteins that are under-carboxylated and biologically inactive, which increases the risk of cardiovascular disease (CVD) and vascular calcification.

Vitamin K2 plays a significant role in maintaining cardiovascular health by regulating calcium balance. Its impact on the cardiovascular system is achieved by activating matrix Gla protein, which inhibits the accumulation of calcium in the arteries.

Does vitamin K clear arteries?

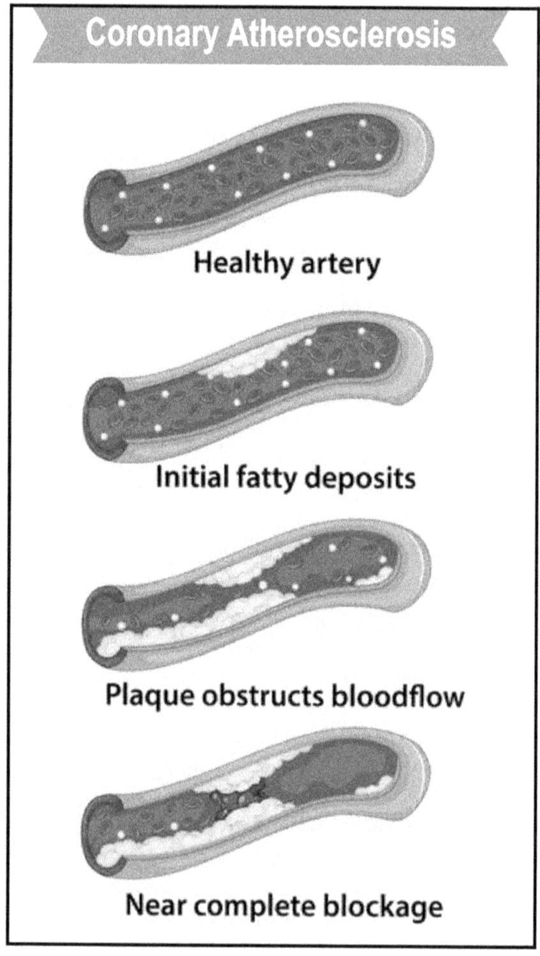

Reviewed by Dr. Gary Gonzalez, MD, in May 2022, and written by Jennifer Ming, a recent study provides compelling evidence that vitamin K2 can slow down the progression of atherosclerosis, a condition where arteries are blocked and can lead to heart attacks and strokes.

- Vitamin K can be obtained from various food sources including green leafy vegetables such as collard greens, turnip greens, kale, spinach, broccoli, Brussels sprouts, and different types of lettuce. Soybean and canola oil as well as salad dressings made with these oils are also good sources of vitamin K. Additionally, fortified meal replacement shakes can be consumed to meet the recommended daily intake of vitamin K.

Minerals

There are various minerals vital for the maintenance of our heart health.

Magnesium is a mineral that occurs naturally in various foods, including dark green vegetables, nuts, and whole grains.

According to Dr. Carolyn Dean, the left ventricle of the heart has the highest magnesium demand compared to any other organ.

Potassium has been recognized for its role in maintaining healthy blood pressure levels, and consuming a diet that is abundant in fruits and vegetables can aid in achieving this goal.

Sodium and potassium function together to signal the cardiac muscles to contract and relax smoothly.

Furthermore, calcium plays a critical role in muscle relaxation and contraction, and is essential for proper nerve function, blood clotting, immune system health, and regulation of blood pressure.

Excess intake of sodium more than 2 grams per day can lead to hypertension and heart disease. A plant-based whole food diet can provide other essential minerals including selenium, cobalt, chromium, manganese, phosphorus, iron, and molybdenum.

- **Nuts, seeds and spices.**

Nuts : Are they good or bad? How much can one consume?

Walnuts Help Keep Our Arteries Clear

Alpha-linoleic acid is known for its anti-inflammatory properties and has been demonstrated to aid in the reduction of plaque formation in coronary arteries. Consumption of walnuts has also been associated with improvement in cholesterol levels and enhanced function of small vessels within the body.

Certain nuts such as Brazils, Macadamias, and cashews contain high amounts of saturated fat, which may lead to arterial blockage and increase the risk of heart attacks over time.

It is important to note that the reader should follow the DiME or Esselstyn program guidelines regarding nuts and seeds. The information provided here is for reference only.

While some physicians may recommend a handful of nuts, patients with coronary disease should avoid this advice as nuts are calorie-dense, and omega-3 fatty acids can easily be obtained from flax seeds.

Seeds: Which ones are good?

Why are flax seeds good for you?

The seed of the flax plant, also known as flaxseed or flax, is a rich source of fiber, protein, potassium, and lignans. Lignans are a type of polyphenol that act as antioxidants, with flaxseed containing 75 to 800 times more lignans than other plant foods, according to Patton. The anti-inflammatory properties of lignans have been demonstrated to prevent heart disease and cancer in various studies.

How to eat flax seeds

According to Patton, flaxseeds are more beneficial when consumed in ground form since the human body has difficulty digesting and absorbing the nutritional content of whole seeds.

Moreover, flaxseeds are high in fiber, and sudden consumption can cause changes in bowel movements, so it is best to introduce it slowly. Studies have demonstrated health benefits with as little as 1 tablespoon of flaxseed per day.

Why are chia seeds beneficial for you?

Chia seeds, like flaxseeds, are a great plant-based source of alpha-linolenic acid, and omega-3 fatty acids.

According to Patton, chia seeds have the added benefit of being able to absorb up to 10 times their weight in water, which makes them useful as a vegan egg substitute. This high water-absorption capacity and fiber content can also help you feel full for a longer time.

How are chia seeds consumed?

To make a lightweight chia gel, mix 1 tablespoon of chia seeds with 1/4 cup of water, and let it sit for about 10 minutes.

Due to their high fiber content, it is recommended to start with just one tablespoon.

Why are pumpkin seeds good for you?

As per Patton, pumpkin seeds, also known as pepitas, are an excellent source of many minerals, including zinc. Zinc has immune-boosting properties.

In addition, research has demonstrated that pumpkin seeds can aid in lowering LDL, or "bad," cholesterol and also prevent muscle weakness.

How are pumpkin seeds eaten?

Pumpkin seeds offer versatility and can be eaten shelled or unshelled, with unshelled seeds containing more fiber. However, it is important to be mindful of portion sizes, as pumpkin seeds are high in fiber, calories, and fat.

Consuming too much in one sitting may cause discomfort such as gas and bloating, and overindulging frequently can lead to weight gain. A cup of pumpkin seeds contains 285 calories, 12 grams of fiber, and 12 grams of fat.

Why are sunflower seeds healthy?

Patton says that sunflower seeds contain many minerals, B vitamins, and antioxidants such as vitamin E and selenium, which help to reduce the level of free radicals in the body.

Free radicals are damaging chemicals that may increase the risk of developing heart disease, diabetes, and certain cancers.

How can one eat sunflower seeds?

Sunflower seeds are available with or without shells. If you choose to eat the shelled variety, simply discard the shells after biting them off.

Why are hemp seeds beneficial to you?

Hemp seeds, also known as hemp hearts, are abundant in potassium and vitamin E. They are an exceptional source of protein among all the seeds and contain healthy omega-6 and omega-3 fats.

How are hemp seeds eaten?

Hemp seeds are larger and crunchier than flax seeds and chia seeds, making them a great addition to salads for added texture.

They can also be sprinkled on rice or vegetables for an extra boost of flavor.

Why are sesame seeds good for you?

Sesame seeds are not only rich in minerals and fiber but also contain high levels of selenium, which is an antioxidant that has been demonstrated to lower the risk of chronic illnesses.

How do you eat sesame seeds?

Sesame seeds can be used as a flavorful addition to Asian inspired dishes, either by using sesame oil or sprinkling the seeds as a garnish. They also add a great texture and taste to salads, quinoa, or rice dishes.

The potential risks of seed-eating

If one is suffering from diverticulitis, it is better to steer clear of consuming seeds.

This is because seeds are high in fiber and may cause bowel irritation.

In addition, seeds can get lodged in the polyps (small growths) in your colon.

It is important to remember that even though they are small, seeds are calorie-dense, so it is best to consume them in moderation to avoid consuming inadvertently excessive calories.

Spices

Spices are a valuable source of antioxidants and scientific research indicates that they possess strong properties in preventing tissue damage and inflammation caused by elevated levels of circulating lipids and blood sugar. Due to their low calorie content and affordability, spices serve as a dependable source of antioxidants and other bioactive compounds in the diet. This review highlights the significance of certain Indian kitchen spices in maintaining a healthy heart, as they are known for their distinct flavors and have the potential to promote cardiovascular health.

Garlic has been recommended as a preventive measure against heart disease. Epidemiological studies have demonstrated a negative correlation between garlic intake and the advancement of cardiovascular disease, which is linked to various factors,

such as raised serum total cholesterol, elevated LDL and an increase in LDL oxidation, increased platelet aggregation, hypertension, and smoking. Garlic is known to inhibit enzymes involved in lipid synthesis, decrease platelet aggregation, prevent lipid peroxidation of oxidized erythrocytes and LDL, increase antioxidant status, and inhibit angiotensin-converting enzyme. Additionally, allicin, an active compound found in garlic, has been shown to significantly reduce the formation of fatty streaks in the aortic sinus.

Curcumin, a spice and medicinal herb used in ancient traditional medicinal systems such as Siddha and Ayurveda for over 5000 years, has various health benefits. Turmeric, containing curcumin, when added to the diet at 1% or 5%, significantly reduces cholesterol and triglyceride levels and increases HDL cholesterol levels within 4 weeks. There is more evidence suggesting that it can decrease LDL oxidation, blood glucose levels, and renal lesions in diabetes. Moreover, it has been shown to lower platelet aggregation, cyclooxygenase, thromboxane, smooth muscle cell proliferation, and endothelial dysfunction.

Turmeric and curcumin are known for their antioxidant and anti-inflammatory properties that have been found to alleviate several health conditions such as pancreatitis, myocardial infarctions, chronic inflammatory lung diseases, inflammatory bowel diseases, hepatic and lung damages, neurodegenerative diseases, as well as cystic fibrosis and muscle injuries. Ginger contains gingerol, an active compound that is believed to have the ability to relax blood vessels, promote blood circulation, and alleviate pain. Furthermore, ginger possesses anti-inflammatory properties that may be beneficial in combating arthritis, heart disease, Alzheimer's disease, and cancer. Studies have also suggested that ginger has antimicrobial, anti-inflammatory, antithrombotic and anticancer effects.

Black pepper is a widely used spice in both Eastern and Western cuisine, offering impressive antioxidant and antibacterial effects, as well as aiding in digestion and weight loss by promoting the breakdown of fat cells. Additionally, it contains vanadium, which has been shown to promote cardiac functional recovery in both myocardial infarction and pressure overload-induced ventricular hypertrophy.

Cinnamon has been found to increase coronary blood flow and improve lipid profile by significantly reducing total cholesterol, triglycerides, and LDL-C levels while increasing serum HDL-C levels. It inhibits the activity of HMG-CoA reductase in the liver, leading to reduced cholesterol levels.

Cinnamon activates PPARγ, leading to improved insulin resistance and a reduction in fasted LDL-c, which helps manage obesity-related hyperlipidemia. Additionally, cinnamon increases NO levels, with NO being a potent vasodilator.

Coriandrum sativum, commonly known as coriander, has been used in traditional medicine to treat patients with high cholesterol and diabetes. The seeds of coriander have a remarkable hypolipidemic effect, lowering lipid levels in the blood. Moreover, extracts from coriander leaf spice are full of natural antioxidants, exhibiting high antiplatelet activity.

The list of spices mentioned above is extensive and will be further elaborated in future editions of this book. However, it is sufficient to mention here that the spices mentioned above have the potential to aid in reversing heart disease.

Antioxidants

Antioxidants are naturally occurring compounds found in foods and produced in the body. They play a crucial role in protecting cells from oxidative stress damage caused by potentially harmful molecules called free radicals.

Spinach, potatoes, broccoli, and carrots are among the vegetables that are high in antioxidants. Other vegetables such as cabbage, artichokes, avocados, asparagus, beetroot, lettuce, radish, squash, sweet potatoes, collard greens, pumpkin, and kale are also good sources of antioxidants. When it comes to fruits, blueberries have the highest antioxidant properties, followed by pomegranates and grapes.

- **Supplements - to take or avoid?**

Vegetarians especially vegans are at a higher risk of developing a deficiency in vitamin B12. This deficiency can lead to an increase in homocysteine levels, which can exacerbate the formation of blockages in the heart. Vitamin B12 can be obtained from a variety of sources, including:

Vegetarian

Soy and almond milk are not naturally rich sources of vitamin B12, but they are often fortified to provide this important nutrient. One cup of soy or almond milk typically contains

2.1 mcg of vitamin B12. Another source of vitamin B12 is nori, a type of dried edible seaweed commonly consumed in Asian countries like Japan. Studies suggest that consuming 4 grams of dried nori daily is enough to meet the daily requirement of vitamin B12.

Some foods are often claimed to be high in vitamin B12, such as unwashed organic produce, mushrooms grown in B12-rich soils, spirulina, chlorella, and nutritional yeast.

However, it is still advisable to take vitamin B12 supplements to ensure that you do not suffer from its deficiency. There are several plant-based vitamin B12 supplement capsules available in the market for this purpose.

Non-vegetarian

Items like meat and dairy that are prohibited, are rich in vitamin B12.

Vegans may also face concerns in reference to their Vitamin D intake. However, sunlight exposure for 20 minutes daily can be a solution to this problem.

In addition to sunlight, sources of Vitamin D include milk, eggs, fatty fish and seafood, oranges, spinach, bananas, mushrooms, and soy milk.

We advise our patients to include vegan sources of vitamin.

D in their diet, or alternatively take a weekly dose of 60K iu to address any deficiency. In cases of insufficient vitamin B12 levels, we recommend a B complex supplement containing.

B1-12 for a period of 3 months until levels normalize, after which we can explore dietary management options.

One must note that the benefits of this diet are not limited to heart patients; anyone can adopt it as a preventive measure and potentially reduce their risk of a heart attack.

During the peak of the Covid-19 pandemic, we observed an increase in the number of heart disease patients and heart attacks, which was partially attributed to Vitamin D deficiency and the prothrombotic nature of the SARS-CoV-2 virus.

In summary, for vegans, B12 and Vitamin D supplements are the only two additional supplements that may be necessary.

Chapter 8

Meditation: Which Style?

Osho

Dynamic meditation is a popular active meditation created by the Indian mystic Osho in 1970. It consists of five stages: deep, fast, chaotic breathing, catharsis, using a mantra "Hoo", silence, and dancing. The key to meditation is watching your mind without any interference. Just observe whatever your mind is doing without judgment or manipulation.

Vipassana

Vipassana is an ancient technique of meditation from India that's emphasizes self-observation and self transformation. It was introduced over 2500 years ago as a remedy for various problems in life. This practice involves disciplined attention to physical sensations, which allows one to directly experience the deep connection between the mind and body. Vipassana has been passed down from generation to generation by a chain of teachers since the time of Buddha.

Pranayama

What is Pranayama Meditation?

Pranayama is the practice of controlling and prolonging one's breath, which enhances conscious awareness of breathing and helps to reshape breathing habits and patterns. On the other hand, meditation is a yogic technique that promotes deep relaxation by allowing the mind to settle into a peaceful state.

We teach a simple and effective technique called **DiME meditation** that can be done anywhere and anytime. Our focus is on breathing, which involves counting the respiratory cycles.

Each respiratory cycle consists of one inspiration and one expiration.

You can sit comfortably in a cross-legged position on the floor, or sit erect on a chair, or even lie down in a corpse pose (savasana).

During this practice, you must use self- affirmations to make your heart healthy. Also conscious awareness for your breath will calm your mind and provide deep rest to all your systems.

Chapter 9

Specific Exercises For Heart Patients

We highly recommend individuals (and patients) to engage in group exercises, as it helps them to stay motivated and on track. However, if someone has a strong mind and will, they can also do it alone, although it is uncommon.

Anti gravity exercises

We observed that anti-gravity exercises, such as lifting arms above the head or cycling legs and arms in the air while lying on the back, resulted in significant benefits for patients. Blood sugar levels dropped from 200 to 150 milligrams per deciliter in several cases within 15 minutes. Similarly, a powerful anti-gravity exercise for type 2 diabetics with heart disease involves sitting on a chair with toes fixed to the ground, and raising and dropping the heels about 3 to 6 inches off the ground for minimum 100 repetitions.

We strongly recommend incorporating the above exercises into your daily routine for optimal results.

Heart Specific yoga

Yoga can harmonize your mind and body through its various components such as Yogasana, Pranayama, Mudras, Savasana, and meditation. While we have covered Pranayama and Savasana in the meditation part, yoga is a simple practice that requires discipline, repetition, and perseverance to achieve maximum benefits with minimal effort. Correct poses should be done gradually, using minimal energy to attain maximum results. Yoga can be done anywhere, whether at home, in the garden, or in a studio, either alone or in a group. It is recommended to keep the stomach empty for a gap of at least two hours before and after yoga, as it is a detoxifying activity.

1. Vruksasana or The Tree pose, is beneficial for heart patients as it involves standing tall and touching the hands above the head.

2. Surya Namaskar, also known as the Sun Salutation, consists of 12 positions and is a complete exercise for the whole body.

3. Swastikasana involves sitting cross-legged comfortably with hands relaxed on the knees.

4. Padmasana, or the Lotus pose, involves sitting cross legged with ankles placed over the opposite thighs.

5. Vajrasana involves sitting erect with bent knees and sitting on the buttocks with a straight neck, head, and torso.

   It helps to reduce visceral fat and improves type 2 diabetes.

6. Uttan Pada Asana is crucial for the abdomen and reducing belly fat and metabolic syndrome.

7. Pawanmuktasana improves the digestive system and reduces angina after a meal.

8. Utkatasana is helpful for thigh muscles and abdomen.

   It aids in improving blood circulation.

9. Pada Hastasana strengthens the heart and improves ejection fraction.

10. Trikonasana, or the side-bending pose, reduces fat in the side abdomen and improves the TOFI syndrome by removing visceral fat.

Our patients have experienced benefits from specific Mudras that are known to be useful for heart problems.

1. Apan Vayu Mudra, where the middle and ring fingers touch the tip of the thumb.

2. Aakash Mudra, where the middle finger and thumb are joined at their tips.

3. Hriday Mudra, where the index finger touches the base of the thumb, and the tip of the thumb touches the tip of the middle and ring fingers, while the little finger is free.

4. Ganesh Mudra, where the fists are closed and the tips of the fingers clench each other.

5. Mukula Mudra, where the fingers touch each other and form a spout-like shape.

6. Padma Mudra, where the thumbs meet each other and the little fingers meet, while the other three fingers are separate.

7. Matangi Mudra, where the ring finger is vertical and touching each other, while the other fingers are clasping/bending to each other.

This book cannot showcase all the images of various yoga Asanas and Mudras due to its limited scope. One can refer to any standard book on yoga and Mudra, or conduct an internet search using Google to access them.

Precautions to take before practicing yoga:

1. Avoid practicing yoga on a full stomach, except in the case of Vajrasana.

2. Avoid practicing yoga forcefully or aggressively. The movements should be slow and controlled for optimal benefit.

3. It is not recommended to practice yoga in dark or noisy environments that may distract one's senses.

Chapter 10

Summary

The DiME program aims for 100% satisfaction. We even have a warranty policy in place for those patients who do not adhere to this program after 3 weeks or who cannot continue in this program due to personal reasons. Here, we have a detailed discussion with that patient and let him choose accordingly.

Extra Value for readers

To make it 100% beneficial, we have also provided the following:

1. Sample Diet plan

   (www.drsureshbhagia.com/DiMEdiet.pdf)

2. Sample Meditation plan

   (www.desureshbhagia.com/DiMEmeditation.pdf)

3. Sample exercise plan

   (www.drsureshbhagia.com/DiMEexercise.pdf)

Bad habits

There are certain addictions and bad habits that lead to heart diseases, and other lifestyle diseases. Smoking is one of the worst chronic habits that surely lead to heart and lung problems. There is nicotine in cigarettes which leads to heart blockages. Since these elements are addictive, it often becomes difficult for people to stop them. But, today, there are different ways of stopping this habit. For example: Pseudo nicotine tablets and dermal patch gives an equivalent satisfaction similar to smoking cigarettes or creates an aversion.

Red wine contains resveratrol supposed to improve ischemic heart disease. We can get this from different sources such as black grapes or red grapes, which impart the same satisfaction.

Beer is supposed to produce a beer belly. Due to the high glucose content, it creates sugar spikes and creates a diabetes like state.

Various types or brands of alcohol also reduce enzymatic action and like Shakespeare says it provoketh the desire and taketh away the performance. Alcohol creates clouding of judgment as well as damage to the internal organs like the liver and stomach and brain.

Tobacco has also been linked to heart disease and it creates inflammatory factors in the endothelial lining of the coronary arteries. Nicotine causes hypertension and creates more friction in the inner lining of the coronary arteries. Carbon monoxide also hampers oxygenation of the heart. Nicotine causes coronary spasm. Also nicotine causes an increase in the heart rate and thus causes angina in smokers.

Disclaimer

This book is entirely dedicated to its readers. Irrespective of the reader being a heart patient or a normal layman, this book will add knowledge in your life and inspire you to lead a heart healthy life.

The results of the DiME program will vary from person to person. It is not the same in everyone's case. In a way, this program will benefit every person who is willing and is serious about bringing a transformation or change in one's life. The program will aid in reversing every chronic problem or lifestyle diseases.

The biggest advantage of pursuing this program is that there are no side effects. DiME works in an unidirectional way creating positive effects only. The program is natural and based on a plant based diet. Our program also includes exercises that are easy to follow and pursue. Thus the mindset is changed towards healing in a holistic way.

People who are already following the DiME program are being monitored and scrutinized properly.

The DiME program does not patronize any groups or corporate companies. It is managed solely by Bhagia Heartcare

PLC. We are *neither for nor against* any other groups of individuals or companies running similar programs.

Any resemblance, partly, in content or methods to similar groups or programs is purely coincidental.

We combine Naturopathy with Allopathy and even Ayurveda and to some extent homeopathy incorporating all the medical sciences to make it beneficial to the patient so as to align the mind, body and spirit in unison.

DiME

Starter Diet sample

www.drsureshbhagia.com/DiMEdiet.pdf

First week diet

Early morning

- 6 am.
- Lemon water-10 ml or sea buckthorn juice 10 ml. or apple cider vinegar - 10 ml. To add water = 500 ml.
- 8 am.
- Wheat grass powder 5 gm. or alfalfa powder 5 gm. Or spirulina powder - 5 gms. To add water = 500 ml.
- 9 am.
- 2 almonds and 2 walnuts

Breakfast

- 11 am.
- Flax seeds or chia seeds or sesame seeds = 1 spoonful.

Lunch

- 1 pm.
- Green juice = 2 glasses

- Or eat raw green leaves 100 grams each of spinach, mint, fenugreek, and coriander.
- 3 pm.
- Half an apple plus half a pear or one orange or one banana.
- 5 pm.
- Green salad of cucumber, bottle gourd, beetroot, carrot, radish, bell pepper

Dinner

- 6 pm.
- Small serving of green leaves and green salad. Plus one satvik roti or multigrain flatbread plus one bowl of vegetable curry or one bowl of daal/lentils.
- 8 pm.
- Lemon water or coconut water.

Monitor your baseline pulse, BP, and blood sugar levels on the commencement of DiME and again two weeks later.

NB: Please note that patients on blood thinners like warfarin after heart valve surgery should avoid excessive green leafy vegetables, as otherwise their clotting tendency will increase. Also patients with calcium oxalate renal stones should avoid too many greens, as their stones will get exacerbated. An expert heart surgeon with dietary knowledge or an experienced nutrition team can guide the patients individually for a tailor made holistic healing program.

We advocate OMAD or one meal a day, for the first month to get faster results.

All milk products are banned for at least two months.

Inflammatory foods like gluten containing wheat are forbidden.

DiME Starter meditation sample

www.drsureshbhagia.com/DiMEmeditation.pdf

Sit erect on a mat or a chair. Close your eyes. Focus your attention on your breathing.

Start counting. One count means one complete cycle of respiration, that is inhalation and exhalation.

Continue until you reach 100 counts or more.

During inspiration, as you breathe inward through your nose, imagine that positive energy is going in and health is coming into your body.

During expiration, as you breathe out, think that your disease is going out. Imagine that your coronary artery blockage or plaque is coming out of your body and melting away.

Positive affirmations and chanting in this manner in sync with your breathing will help in resolving your heart disease.

Gradually, the coronary artery disease will reduce in significance.

Love yourself. Love your body. Focus your mind on your heart.

DiME Starter Exercise Sample

www.drsureshbhagia.com/DiMEexercise.pdf

- Do these Yoga Asanas daily for 20 minutes and mudras for 7 minutes.
- 10 Asanas, each about 2 minutes.
- 7 Mudras, each held for 1 minute.

Asanas are to be done slowly, to sustain the position, and then let go at ease.

1. Vruks Asana 1 minute
2. Surya Namaskar 6 rounds 3 minutes
3. Swastik Asana 2 minutes
4. Padma Asana 2 minutes
5. Vajra Asana 2 minutes
6. Uttanpada Asana 2 minutes
7. Pawanmukt Asana 2 minutes
8. Utkat Asana 2 minutes
9. Padahasta Asana 2 minutes
10. Trikon Asana 2 minutes

Mudras are to be performed in the right form and position.

1. Apan Vayu
2. Akash

3. Hriday
4. Ganesh
5. Mukula
6. Padama
7. Matangi

Author's Personal Experience

/2/my-drive

Consultant Pathologist

928-909-0609 ccsupport@redcliffelabs.com www.redcliffelabs.com

Redcliffe Lifetech Pvt. Ltd. (Unit of Redcliffe Lifetech Inc, USA) **Plot No. 144/C, Ground Floor, Chandrasekharpur, Bhubaneswar, District - Khordha, Pin - 751016**

All Lab results are subject to clinical interpretation by qualified medical professional and this report is not subject to use for any medico-legal purpose.

21-Aug-2022 07:02 PM Page 10 of 12

LABORATORY REPORT

Patient NAME	: **Mr SURESH BHAGIA**	Bill DATE	: Aug 20, 2022, 04:16 PM
DOB/Age/Gender	: Male	Sample Collected	: Aug 20, 2022, 07:00 AM
Patient ID / UHID	: 1338887/352965	Sample Received	: Aug 21, 2022, 07:57 AM
Referred BY	: Dr	Report DATE	: Aug 21, 2022, 06:59 PM
Sample TYPE	: Serum	BarcodeNo	: BC651039
CLIENT	:	Report STATUS	: Final Report

Test Description	**Value(s)**	**Unit(s)**	**Reference Range**
	BIOCHEMISTRY REPORT		
	RW2		
	C Peptide		
C-PEPTIDE FASTING, SERUM Method : ECLIA	2.21	ng/mL	1.1 - 4.4

Interpretation:
Clinical Use

- Assess pancreatic islet cell function
- Distinguish insulin secreting tumors (Insulinoma) from exogenous insulin administration as a cause of hypoglycemia (commercial insulin does not contain C-peptide). Sera from Insulinoma patients have high insulin and high C-peptide levels whereas hypoglycemia from injected or exogenous insulin shows high insulin and low C-peptide levels.
- Distinguish Type I and Type II Diabetes mellitus

Increased Levels – Insulinoma & Type II Diabetes

Decreased Levels- Type I Diabetes & Exogenous insulin administration

/my-drive

LABORATORY REPORT

9001 :2015

X labs

Patient NAME	: **Mr SURESH BHAGIA**	Bill DATE	: Aug 20, 2022, 04:16 PM
DOB/Age/Gender	: /Male	Sample Collected	: Aug 20, 2022, 07:00 AM
Patient ID / UHID	: 1338887/352965	Sample Received	: Aug 21, 2022, 07:57 AM
Referred BY	: Dr.	Report DATE	: Aug 21, 2022, 01:16 PM
Sample TYPE	: Serum	BarcodeNo	: BC651039
CLIENT	:	Report STATUS	: Final Report

Test Description	Value(s)	Unit(s)	Reference Range
BIOCHEMISTRY REPORT			
RW2			
Insulin Fasting			
Insulin (Fasting) Method : CMIA	7.8	µU/mL	<25.0

Interpretation:

Note

1. A single random blood sample for insulin may provide insufficient information due to wide variation in the time responses of insulin levels and blood glucose.
2. Stimulation of insulin secretion may be caused by many factors like hyperglycemia, glucagon, amino acids, growth hormone and catecholamines.
3. Interference in insulin assay is seen due to insulin antibodies which develop in patients treated with bovine or porcine insulin.

Clinical Utility

- Evaluation of fasting hypoglycemia
- Evaluation of Polycystic Ovary syndrome
- Classification of Diabetes mellitus
- Predict Diabetes mellitus
- Assessment of Beta cell activity
- Select optimal therapy for Diabetes
- Investigation of insulin resistance
- Predict the development of Coronary Artery Disease

Increased levels - Insulinoma, Some Type II diabetic patients, Infantile hypoglycemia, Hyperinsulinism, Obesity, Cushing's syndrome, Oral contraceptives, Acromegaly, Hyperthyroidism

Decreased levels - Untreated Type I Diabetes mellitus

/2/my-drive

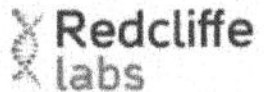

Patient NAME	: **Mr SURESH BHAGIA**	Bill DATE	: Aug 20, 2022, 04:16 PM
DOB/Age/Gender	Male	Sample Collected	: Aug 20, 2022, 07:00 AM
Patient ID / UHID	: 1338887/352965	Sample Received	: Aug 20, 2022, 04:16 PM
Referred BY	: Dr	Report DATE	: Aug 20, 2022, 06:10 PM
Sample TYPE	: Serum	BarcodeNo	: BC651039
CLIENT	:	Report STATUS	: Final Report

Test Description	Value(s)	Unit(s)	Reference Range
BIOCHEMISTRY REPORT			
RW2			
High Sensitivity C-Reactive Protein (Hs-CRP)			
HIGHLY SENSITIVE C-REACTIVE PROTEIN (hs-CRP) Method : Turbidimetric/Immunoturbidimetry	**0.1**	mg/L	Low < 1.00 mg/L Average 1.0-3.0 mg/L High > 3.0 mg/L

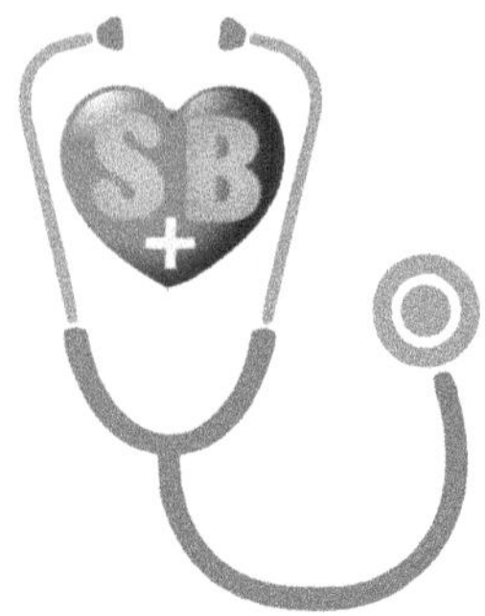

Dr. Suresh Bhagia

Join us to Celebrate 2023: Year of the Millets@India

To Connect, Comment and Collaborate:

Tel. +91 9484821130

Email: heartdoctorsb@gmail.com

www.drsureshbhagia.com

Ahmedabad, Gujarat, India

+91 7600860606

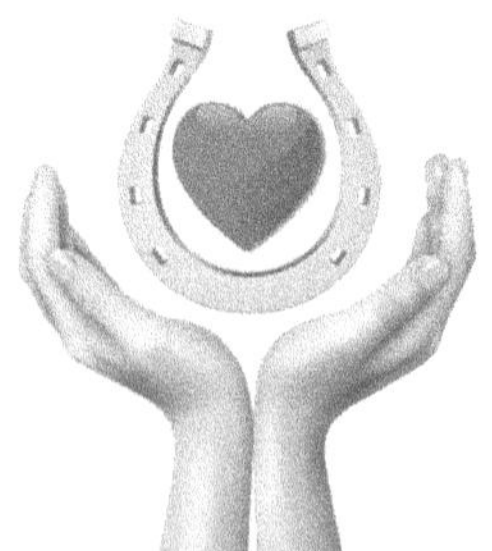

Bhagia Heartcare PLC

www.ingramcontent.com/pod-product-compliance
Ingram Content Group UK Ltd.
Pitfield, Milton Keynes, MK11 3LW, UK
UKHW021656190726
13853UKWH00001B/306